ASHES TO FIRE

DAILY REFLECTIONS FROM ASH WEDNESDAY TO PENTECOST

EDITED BY
MERRITT J. NIELSON

BEACON HILL PRESS
OF KANSAS CITY

Copyright 2010 by Beacon Hill Press of Kansas City
ISBN 978-0-8341-2592-6

Printed in the
United States of America

Cover and Interior Design: Imago Studios

10 9 8 7 6 5 4 3 2 1

CONTENTS

THE APOSTLES' CREED

I believe in God the Father Almighty,
maker of heaven and earth;
And in Jesus Christ his only Son, our Lord;
who was conceived by the Holy Spirit,
born of the Virgin Mary, suffered under Pontius Pilate,
was crucified, dead, and buried;
he descended into hell;
the third day he rose again from the dead;
he ascended into heaven,
and sitteth on the right hand of God,
the Father Almighty;
from thence he shall come to judge the living
and the dead.
I believe in the Holy Spirit,
the holy catholic church,
the communion of saints,
the forgiveness of sins,
the resurrection of the body,
and the life everlasting.
Amen.

A Journey with Jesus from Ash Wednesday to Pentecost

*F*aithful followers of Jesus yearn for deep spiritual renewal. They hunger for a more meaningful relationship with God. This desire to draw closer to God inspires them to read Scripture, fast, and pray. But often the excitement about having such a life of devotion is dampened by not knowing where to begin or how to keep going.

Ashes to Fire is simply one way to get started in a sustained devotional life. It accomplishes this by following the Christian calendar, a practice that has helped the church for centuries keep its focus on the three great festival days--Christmas, Easter, and Pentecost.

As a gentle but purposeful guide, Ashes to Fire invites us into the deeper life by taking us on an intense journey with Jesus: from Ash Wednesday through Holy Week and Easter, and then on to Pentecost--from penitence, to praise, to power. Week by week and day by day our anticipation will rise as we draw closer to the celebration of Easter and then continue on to that of Pentecost. This third great festival of the church captures Easter's exuberance, along with a joy-filled recognition of God's presence and purifying power among us. As with Easter, here is an opportunity for the church to rejoice with inspiring music and to remember with story. It can tell again about the outpouring of the Spirit in fullness and power, the promised gift of Jesus to his people.

Along with the journey to Pentecost, Ashes to Fire offers a combination of Bible reading, spiritual reflection, and prayer that could, if followed faithfully, be an avenue to God's transforming, life-renewing power. Prayerfully immersing ourselves in the Sacred Scriptures is one way to satisfy our hunger to know Christ in a deeper, more intimate way. John, in remembering the words of Jesus, gives us a key insight: "You search the scriptures because you think that in them you have eternal life; and it is they that testify on my behalf" (John 5:39). The best way to deepen our relationship with the Living Word is to spend time in reading and meditating on the Written Word. *Ashes to Fire* provides just such an opportunity.

While there are several companion Ashes to Fire resources available for use in the local church (www.ashestofire.org), this devotional guide is the heart and soul of the journey. Here are the compass points for those who want to join others on this pilgrimage and rehearse with them the stories of our faith. In addition, participants will find inspirational music written specifically for the biblical theme of each Sunday of the Ashes to Fire experience on the CD included with this book, along with the theme song, "Ashes to Fire" (CD-Track 15).

THE LENTEN AND EASTER SEASONS

The season of Lent begins with Ash Wednesday and continues for 6 weeks. Palm Sunday, the 6th Sunday of Lent, marks the beginning of Holy Week, which concludes on Holy Saturday, the day before Easter Sunday, or Resurrection Day. The first Sunday of Easter marks the beginning of the season of Easter, 50 days that lead up to Pentecost Sunday. In total, these 14 weeks will give shape and substance to our spiritual adventure; and in the spirit of the literary classic *Canterbury Tales,* we have 14 stories from the Gospels to be retold and remembered along the way—historical accounts from the life of the Savior that we will consider in depth as we walk the pilgrim pathway together toward Pentecost.

Using the Ashes to Fire Devotional and Study Guide

THE LENTEN PRELUDE

Ash Wednesday begins our Ashes to Fire experience. We start with a brief explanation of the day's significance and a devotional reflection on the call to repentance and renewal both from the ancient prophets and from our Lord himself. The next three days follow a pattern of personal daily devotions, as explained below in the section titled Monday through Saturday Personal Devotional Guide.

SUNDAY DEVOTIONAL REFLECTION FOR GROUP STUDY

Each Sunday, a devotional reflection based on a key Gospel narrative provides a background resource for Sunday school class conversations or small-group study. In addition to reading the Gospel passage and the devotional reflection, you should also read the suggested companion passages, usually one from the Old Testament, one from the Psalms, and one from the New Testament Epistles. Discussion prompts help to prepare you for participation in your group discussions. Use your reflective journaling section to record any other insights that come to you as you read and think about the passages or the devotional reflection. When the 14 weeks are over, you will have a personal diary of your spiritual journey to keep for later reference.

MONDAY THROUGH SATURDAY PERSONAL DEVOTIONAL GUIDE

Each day of the 14-week period includes a personal devotional guide that begins with a brief prayer, followed by four suggested readings for the day—one from the Old Testament, one from the Psalms, one from the Epistles, and one from the Gospels. If you do not have the time to read these passages in their entirety, each of the first three is briefly summarized for you. It is suggested that you always read the daily Gospel lesson in its entirety (the scripture quotations are from the New Revised Standard Version). Also included in the daily guide are inspirational quotes from men and women of faith who keep us connected with our shared Christian heritage. In the evening, an excerpt from the Psalms and a brief prayer provide preludes to nighttime rest and renewal. Prayers marked with a **JW** icon are based on John Wesley's Forms of Prayer.

One church leader of the 20th century, Dr. J. B. Chapman, concluded his book *The Terminology of Holiness* with these words:

> We know in truth the spiritual meaning of the fire-
> touched lips of Isaiah. Even the holy apostles who walked
> with the Master in the days of His flesh were taught to
> look forward to the fullness of the Spirit's baptism, which
> is the normal heritage of all God's people . . . to be filled
> with the love of God; to have His love made perfect in
> our hearts; there is nothing better than this.

The goal of Ashes to Fire is to help every believer know "in truth the spiritual meaning" of such power and purity, of a heart filled to capacity with the burning love of God. Perhaps the book you hold in your hands will provide the answer to your own soul's longings for a relationship with the Lord that will forever change your life. God be with you, pilgrim. Let's take the journey together.

For the Ashes to Fire Team
Merritt J. Nielson
Curriculum Director

We acknowledge our debt of gratitude to our primary writers for this personal devotional guide: Shane Ash, John Bowling, Robert Broadbooks, Russell F. Metcalfe Jr., Jeren Rowell, Woodie Stevens, and J. K. Warrick. Please visit www.ashestofire.org for other resources, including Sunday school and small-group discussion guides for children, youth, and adults; sermon and worship suggestions; and music for public services and personal listening.

LENTEN SEASON

Ash Wednesday:
With Jesus at the Place of Repentance

Read the passages from Joel 2 and Matthew 6:1-6, 16-21,
the introductory reflection, "Dust Thou Art," and then
the additional devotional material for the day.

THE MUSIC OF ASHES TO FIRE

Prelude Days: "Burn Away" (Track 1)

Thursday through Saturday

IN THE MORNING:

A personal daily devotional guide includes prayer,
a reading from the Old Testament, the Psalms, the Epistles,
and the Gospel for each day of the week.

The Bible readings for the Lenten Prelude
are from Deuteronomy, Titus, and the Gospel of John.

Inspirational quotes from men and women of faith
keep us in contact with our shared Christian heritage.

IN THE EVENING:

An evening psalm and prayer become preludes
to nighttime rest and renewal.

LENTEN SEASON–THE PRELUDE
With Jesus at the Place of Repentance

**A devotional reflection based on Joel 2:1-2, 12-17;
Matthew 6:1-6, 16-21**

Dust Thou Art

"*Dust thou art,*" goes some of the ritual associated with today, "*and to dust thou shalt return!*" That may not be an uplifting thought, but then we are reminded that Ash Wednesday is where the journey begins—again. It is the first day of a pilgrimage that began a long time ago, a journey that believers have been taking for centuries. Together, committed followers of Jesus are invited to walk with him to Jerusalem and the cross.

Ash Wednesday is a wake-up call that life is transient. The words the pastor speaks and the scriptures that we read underscore our humanity, our mortality. The solemnity of the journey is good and necessary. There is no bypassing the cross for those who go this way. This is not a time for careless exuberance. Thankfully, we are not making this journey alone. Jesus walks with us. And so do many, many other brothers and sisters in Christ all around the world. We are in the best of company even though at times we may feel alone.

Ash Wednesday is a challenge to put our lives in perspective. "Dust thou art" may not be very flattering, but it's something we need to hear. We really are pretty small items in a very large universe. And we go around talking as if we understand who God really is and what God really thinks, and that our navel is the center of the universe and God exists for us—and then this! **"Hello, speck!"** We are brought up short by the fact that we are infinitesimally small. Yet, we try to grasp the paradox that God knows and cares for each one of us.

Ash Wednesday, then, becomes a focus on absolute basics. Our self-indulgent culture would have us believe we cannot live without the things it values. We even think worship is a means to our improvement and well-being. We want what we want and heaven too. Jesus calls us to let him decide what we need and where we go. So Ash Wednesday is the joy of knowing Jesus wants us to walk with him.

Jesus calls us to simplicity, to listen. Don't be too quick to set goals or make arbitrary decisions about giving things up for Lent. Instead, maybe we need to start by giving up explaining what we think we need. More often than not, prayer should be more listening, less talking. Silence is golden, precious and hard to come by.

Jesus calls us to self-denial. *Self*-denial ultimately is just that: denying *one-self* in favor of someone (Someone) else's decision. It is giving up my way and agreeing to go God's way. Often we think of self-denial as giving up chocolate or Facebook or some time-consuming pastime so we can be reminded of our purpose and spend more quiet time in prayer and meditation. Probably that is a good start. Whatever the level of self-denial, all of them seek to bring us into harmony with God's purpose. God-inspired self-denial will create confidence in praying.

Jesus calls us corporately. Ash Wednesday is a rallying time. The Bible speaks of corporate efforts, of fasting and waiting on God—a corporate longing after God until our times of worship reflect a united willingness to keep going step-by-step to Calvary and beyond.

Observing Ash Wednesday

Where is Ash Wednesday in the Bible? It isn't. But there are plenty of precedents for calling God's people together for repentance, for fresh anointings, and for renewal. The trumpet sound of the prophet Joel, calling for God's people to tremble at the approaching judgments of God (Joel 2:1-2,12-17) resonates with the call of Jesus to times of mourning and calling on God with self-denial and even fasting. Notice Jesus does not say "If you fast" but "Whenever you fast . . ." as if he expects us to keep in step with his own example (Matthew 6:1-6, 16-21).

Why ashes? Ashes in the Bible are a sign of mourning or humility before the holiness of God (see Daniel 9:3; Job 42:6; Jonah 3:6; Matthew 11:21).

The Ash Wednesday service for many denominations involves the reading of Scripture, perhaps a very short message outlining the journey to Good Friday, Easter, and beyond. People are then invited to come forward and the pastor marks a small black cross with ashes on each person's forehead. Traditionally these ashes are from the burning of the previous Palm Sunday's palms, mixed to a light paste with pure olive oil. Often the service includes Holy Communion.

Do we need to follow a certain ritual? *No, but neither do we need to reinvent the wheel.* If your church wants to begin an Ash Wednesday observance, a good place to start is with discovering what is good in established traditions. We can approach these sacred times that belong to all the church with humility and reverence. In them we can realize an opportunity to deepen our awareness of God's forgiveness and purifying presence. Thus, an <u>Ash Wednesday service invites us to humble ourselves before God as we prepare to follow in the steps of Jesus all the way to Calvary.</u>

Thankfully, the journey doesn't end here. Jesus has promised we can keep on walking with him all the way to Pentecost and beyond, but for the next 14 weeks we will be doing a lot of listening, reading, and praying.

"Dust thou art," goes the graveside ritual, "and to dust thou shalt return!" That may not be an uplifting thought, but then again, as we begin the Lenten season in our Ashes to Fire journey of intensive and intentional fellowship with Jesus, we are reminded that God has done some marvelous things with dust—when the dust yielded to the touch of its Creator. —RFM

REFLECTIVE JOURNALING

_____

_____

_____

_____

_____

_____

_____

_____

_____

_____

_____

PSALM 143 ▪ AMOS 5:6-15 ▪ HEBREWS 12:1-14 ▪ LUKE 18:9-14

MORNING MEDITATIONS

PRAYER—Lord God, send your Holy Spirit to be the guide of all my ways and the sanctifier of my soul and body. Give me the light of your presence, your peace from heaven, and the salvation of my soul, through Jesus Christ my Lord. Amen. *JW*

PSALM 143:1, 5-6—Hear my prayer, O LORD; give ear to my supplications in your faithfulness; answer me in your righteousness . . . I remember the days of old, I think about all your deeds, I meditate on the works of your hands. I stretch out my hands to you; my soul thirsts for you like a parched land.

AMOS 5:14-15 *Love the Good, Establish Justice*
Seek good and not evil, that you may live; and so the LORD, the God of hosts, will be with you, just as you have said. Hate evil and love good, and establish justice in the gate; it may be that the LORD, the God of hosts, will be gracious to the remnant of Joseph.

HEBREWS 12:1b-2 *Run with Perseverance*
Let us run with perseverance the race that is set before us, looking to Jesus the pioneer and perfecter of our faith, who for the sake of the joy that was set before him endured the cross, disregarding its shame, and has taken his seat at the right hand of the throne of God.

LUKE 18:9-14 *Today's Gospel Reading*

Let us fix our thoughts on the blood of Christ; and reflect how precious that blood is in God's eyes, inasmuch as its outpouring for our salvation has opened the grace of repentance to all mankind.   AN EXCERPT FROM CLEMENT'S LETTER TO THE CORINTHIANS

EVENING REFLECTIONS

PSALM 102:1-2—Hear my prayer, O LORD; let my cry come to you. Do not hide your face from me in the day of my distress. Incline your ear to me; answer me speedily in the day when I call.

PRAYER—Father, grant me forgiveness of what is past, that in the days to come I may with a pure spirit, do your will—walking humbly with you, showing love to all, and keeping body and soul in sanctification and honor, in Jesus' name. Amen.

PSALM 37 ▪ **DEUTERONOMY 7:6-11** ▪ **TITUS 1:1-16** ▪ **JOHN 1:29-34**

MORNING MEDITATIONS

PRAYER—Eternal Father, I acknowledge that all I am, all I have is yours. Give me such a sense of your goodness today, that I may return to you all possible love and obedience, in Jesus' name. Amen. *JW*

PSALM 37:7a, 27-28—Be still before the Lord, and wait patiently for him . . . Depart from evil, and do good; so you shall abide forever. For the Lord loves justice; he will not forsake his faithful ones.

DEUTERONOMY 7:6, 11   *His Treasured Possession*
For you are a people holy to the Lord your God; the Lord your God has chosen you out of all the peoples on earth to be his people, his treasured possession . . . therefore, observe diligently the commandment . . . that I am commanding you today.

TITUS 1:1*b*-3   *Grace and Peace*
For the sake of . . . the knowledge of the truth that is in accordance with godliness, in the hope of eternal life that God, who never lies, promised before the ages began—in due time he revealed his word through the proclamation with which I have been entrusted by the command of God our Savior.

JOHN 1:29-34   *Today's Gospel Reading*

Joel speaks of God as "gracious and merciful, slow to anger and abounding in steadfast love" . . . But he did not want us to make the thought of God's great mercy a pretext for careless living . . . For my part, Joel says, I beg of you to repent and I assure you that God's mercy surpasses our wildest dreams.   AN EXCERPT FROM JEROME'S COMMENTARY ON JOEL

EVENING REFLECTIONS

PSALM 37:39-40—The salvation of the righteous is from the Lord; he is their refuge in the time of trouble. The Lord helps them and rescues them; he rescues them from the wicked, and saves them because they take refuge in him.

PRAYER—Lord God, you see my heart, and my desires are not hidden from you. To you, O God, Father, Son and Holy Spirit, my Creator, Redeemer, and Sanctifier, I give up myself entirely. May I no longer serve myself, but you alone. Amen.

PSALM 31 ▪ DEUTERONOMY 7:12-16 ▪ TITUS 2:1-15 ▪ JOHN 1:35-42

MORNING MEDITATIONS

PRAYER—Everlasting God, I bless you with my whole heart and thank you for your goodness to me. Watch over me today with eyes of mercy; direct my soul and body according to your will, and fill my heart with your Holy Spirit that I may live this day, and all the rest of my days, to your glory. Amen. *JW*

PSALM 31:14-15a, 16—But I trust in you, O LORD; I say, "You are my God." My times are in your hand; deliver me . . . Let your face shine upon your servant; save me in your steadfast love.

DEUTERONOMY 7:12-13 *God Will Bless You*
If you heed these ordinances, by diligently observing them, the LORD your God will maintain with you the covenant of loyalty that he swore to your ancestors; he will love you, bless you, and multiply you . . . in the land that he swore to your ancestors to give you.

TITUS 2:11-12 *Live Godly Lives*
For the grace of God has appeared, bringing salvation to all, training us to renounce impiety and worldly passions, and in the present age to live lives that are self-controlled, upright and godly.

JOHN 1:35-42 *Today's Gospel Reading*

Would you honor the body of Christ? Do not honor him here in church clothed in silk vestments and then pass him by unclothed and frozen outside . . . Adorn your house if you will, but do not forget your brother in distress. He is a temple of infinitely greater value.   AN EXCERPT FROM A SERMON BY JOHN CHRYSOSTOM

EVENING REFLECTIONS

PSALM 35:10, 22—O LORD, who is like you? You deliver the weak from those too strong for them, the weak and needy from those who despoil them . . . You have seen, O LORD; do not be silent! O Lord, do not be far from me.

PRAYER—O my God, I love you above all things, with my whole heart and soul, because you are worthy of all my love. I forgive all who have injured me, and I ask pardon for all whom I may have injured. Amen.

PSALM 32 • DEUTERONOMY 7:17-26 • TITUS 3:1-15 • JOHN 1:43-51

MORNING MEDITATIONS

PRAYER—O Lord of Life, put your grace into my heart, that I may worthily magnify your great and glorious name. You have made me and sent me into the world to do your work. Assist me to fulfill the purpose of my creation, and to show your praise by giving up myself to your service, today and always. Amen. *JW*

PSALM 32:1-2, 11—Happy are those whose transgression is forgiven, whose sin is covered. Happy are those to whom the LORD imputes no iniquity, and in whose spirit there is no deceit . . .Be glad in the LORD and rejoice, O righteous, and . . . upright in heart.

DEUTERONOMY 7:18-19 *Remember What the Lord Did*
Do not be afraid . . . Just remember what the LORD your God did to Pharaoh and to all Egypt, the great trials that your eyes saw, the signs and wonders, the mighty hand and the outstretched arm by which the LORD your God brought you out.

TITUS 3:4-5a *He Saved Us*
But when the goodness and loving kindness of God our Savior appeared, he saved us, not because of any works of righteousness that we had done, but according to his mercy.

JOHN 1:43-51 *Today's Gospel Reading*

Happy are we if we put into practice what we hear and sing. For our hearing is a sowing of seed and our actions the fruit of that seed. Having said this, I would warn you against coming into church fruitlessly, hearing such good tidings but not producing good works.

AN EXCERPT FROM A SERMON BY ST. AUGUSTINE

EVENING REFLECTIONS

PSALM 43:3-4a—O send out your light and your truth; let them lead me; let them bring me to your holy hill and to your dwelling. Then I will go to the altar of God, to God my exceeding joy.

PRAYER—O God, you instruct me with your laws, you redeem me by the blood of your Son, and you sanctify me by the grace of your Holy Spirit. Let me rest in peace so that I may rise more fit for service in your kingdom, in Jesus' name. Amen. *JW*

WEEK ONE
LENTEN SEASON

Sunday: With Jesus in the Desert

Read the Gospel passage from Matthew 4:1-11, the devotional
reflection titled "No Shortcuts," and respond to the discussion
prompts in the Reflective Journaling section.

THE MUSIC OF ASHES TO FIRE

Week 1: "Lead Me" (Track 2)

Monday through Saturday of Week 1

IN THE MORNING:

A personal daily devotional guide includes prayer,
a reading from the Old Testament, the Psalms, the Epistles, and
the Gospel for each day of the week.

This week's readings are from Deuteronomy, Hebrews,
and the Gospel of John.

Inspirational quotes from men and women of faith keep us
in contact with our shared Christian heritage.

IN THE EVENING:

An evening psalm and prayer become preludes
to nighttime rest and renewal.

LENTEN SEASON–WEEK ONE
With Jesus in the Desert

A devotional reflection based on Matthew 4:1-11

Read the Gospel passage first, then the devotional reflection that follows. The discussion prompts at the end will help prepare you for Sunday school and small-group sessions.

No Shortcuts

Our first steps with Jesus on our Lenten journey take us to a desert wilderness far from his baptism by John the Baptist. The Spirit has led him away from the crowds and excitement. As we fall into step with him, he has fasted many days. Haggard and drawn, Jesus is confronted with evil offering what appear to be helpful suggestions. But the words have a suspicious ring. The temptation begins innocently enough.

"Make these stones into bread! You're famished. This is the real world. You're not going to survive at this rate! A dead Messiah isn't going to do anyone any good."

It isn't that Jesus isn't hungry. It isn't that he can't work a miracle. Later he will fed five thousand people with a little boy's lunch. Survival isn't the issue. For Jesus, taking orders solely from the Father is what he is all about, so he surely is not going to take advice from the Evil One.

"Man does not live by bread alone," he says, "but by every word that proceeds from the mouth of God."

The sympathetic tone continues, as the temptation steps to another level.

"What is this fasting and praying all about? Excitement is what sells! You need publicity! Put on a show! Do miracles! You can be famous!"

But Jesus is not a performer. He doesn't do things for the effect. It isn't that he can't master the forces of nature. Later he will walk on the sea and calm storms. He will even raise the dead. But his greatest miracle is teaching us to love, to love even the way of the cross. The way to eternal life has no flashy shortcuts. Jesus listens to one Voice only.

"Don't try to make God do tricks!" is his reply.

The third temptation is maybe the most insidious of all. It is the temptation to compromise. The tempter offers to join forces with Jesus, but on his terms.

"A cross is a terrible way to go! No one will see out here in the desert if you just bow down and kneel before me. What does the Father care? What does he know? You have to take charge of your life! Just worship me and you'll have no competition! Be powerful: you need to take charge! Assert yourself!"

Here Jesus, at his weakest, uses the defense that is available to us all as we learn to walk with him in the time of temptation. He doesn't try to reason with the Enemy. He reaches back into the Father's promises. He flees to the first commandment.

"Away with you, Satan!" he cries, "for it is written, 'Worship the Lord your God and serve only him.'"

Satan has to leave. The angels come, there in the wilderness, and Jesus is refreshed. Then he resumes the step-by-step following of the Father's will that will take him to Calvary, to Olivet, and to the glory beyond. There will be no compromise, no shortcut.

With Jesus in the wilderness of temptation we learn to reject the false sympathy of the tempter and dare to be faithful, as he is faithful.

If you are a student, you want good grades. They open doors. They bring scholarships. The easiest way to good grades is to let someone else do your work for you. But there is no real shortcut to genuine education.

If you are lonely, you want intimacy and the good feelings of love and security. No one has to tell you those are good things. The easiest way to those feelings is the pathway of least resistance. But there are no shortcuts to real friendship. There is never an excuse to use people like things, no matter what the goal may be.

If you are ambitious, you want success and influence. Within the boundaries of genuine caring those could be very worthy goals. But in our world, all too often personal goals are reached at whatever the cost. But there is no shortcut to real integrity. Cheating is always wrong; adultery and fornication are always sin; betrayal of confidence is always heartbreaking.

Whatever the reason, remember: there are no shortcuts to finding and doing God's will. It is a wonderful thing to realize that in God's will we don't need shortcuts! He is with us and will help us to do his will, if we only allow him. So there are no shortcuts in walking with Jesus.

A workman went to his big boss one day and said, "I'm tired. I think I'll take my retirement benefits and hang it up. It's been great working for you."

The big boss looked disappointed and said, "I really hate to see you go. I was hoping you could do at least one more big job for me. Will you, just one more?" Reluctantly the builder agreed to build a house for some important client of the big boss.

It was a big house, a big job, a lot of work. It was on a golf course, with a lot of detail. But the man's heart really wasn't in it. He threw the house together in record time and cut corners on material and labor wherever he could. He saved the boss a lot of money, but it wasn't really his best work and he knew it.

Imagine how he felt when he turned the keys over to the big boss and the boss gave them right back and fished around in his briefcase and gave him the title and deed to the property on the golf course.

"This is my gift for you!" he said. "Thanks for all your good work over the years!"

Then the builder wished he hadn't been in such a hurry. He wished he hadn't cut corners and taken shortcuts just to get the job done.

Life is like that. Exactly like that. We become the product of our own integrity in following after God—or our lack of integrity. Either we become exiles from innocence when we try to take shortcuts to being like God, or with the Holy Spirit's help, we walk with Jesus and use the promises and the commandments of God to resist the tempter's power and share in Christ's very life, living in his righteousness.

This is the first Sunday in Lent. The journey is under way. Today is a good time to ask God to give us grace to be like Jesus as we face temptations to cut corners, to take shortcuts, to compromise in any way with the known will of God. I don't know about you, but I don't want to try to get away with building a shoddy house. I know I'm going to have to live in what I build.   —RFM

After reading the passage from Matthew 4 and the devotional reflection "No Shortcuts," you may also want to read the following related passages:
Genesis 2:15-17; 3:1-7; Psalm 32; and Romans 5:12-19

The **discussion prompts** that follow will help prepare you to participate in your Sunday school class or small-group study. Use your **reflective journaling**

section to record any other insights that come to you as you read the Gospel lesson and the devotional reflection.

DISCUSSION PROMPT #1: MATTHEW 4

Matthew describes three different temptations in this passage. What was the nature of each of the three?

DISCUSSION PROMPT #2: MATTHEW 4

What might Jesus have gained by yielding to each temptation? What price would he have paid for giving in to each?

DISCUSSION PROMPT #3: MATTHEW 4

How did Jesus overcome these temptations?

DISCUSSION PROMPT #4: MATTHEW 4

Do these verses only apply to Jesus because he is the Messiah, or can they have meaning for our lives as well? Why?

DISCUSSION PROMPT #5: DEVOTIONAL REFLECTION

The writer of *No Shortcuts* uses an illustration to conclude the devotional reflection. How does that story speak to you? The last sentence?

REFLECTIVE JOURNALING

_____

_____

_____

_____

_____

_____

_____

_____

_____

_____

PSALM 41 ▪ DEUTERONOMY 8:11-20 ▪ HEBREWS 2:11-18 ▪ JOHN 2:1-12

MORNING MEDITATIONS

PRAYER—Almighty God, to you all hearts are open, all desires known, and all secrets exposed; cleanse the thoughts of my heart by the inspiration of your Holy Spirit, that I may perfectly love you and worthily magnify your holy name, through Jesus Christ my Lord. Amen.

PSALM 41:1-2—Happy are those who consider the poor; the LORD delivers them in the day of trouble. The LORD protects them and keeps them alive; they are called happy in the land.

DEUTERONOMY 8:11 *Take Care; Don't Forget*
Take care that you do not forget the LORD your God, by failing to keep his commandments, his ordinances, and his statutes, which I am commanding you today.

HEBREWS 2:17-18 *He Is Able to Help*
Therefore [Jesus] had to become like his brothers and sisters in every respect, so that he might be a merciful and faithful high priest in the service of God, to make a sacrifice of atonement for the sins of the people. Because he himself was tested by what he suffered, he is able to help those who are being tested.

JOHN 2:1-12 *Today's Gospel Reading*

Happy are we if we put into practice what we hear and sing. For our hearing is a sowing of seed and our actions the fruit of that seed   ST. AUGUSTINE, SERMON 23A, 1-4

EVENING REFLECTIONS

PSALM 41:4, 12-13—As for me, I said, "O LORD, be gracious to me; heal me, for I have sinned against you." . . . You have upheld me because of my integrity, and set me in your presence forever. Blessed be the LORD, the God of Israel, from everlasting to everlasting. Amen and Amen.

PRAYER—Be present, O God, and protect us through the silent hours of this night, so that we who are wearied by the changes of this fleeting world may rest in your eternal changless- ness, in the name of Christ, I pray. Amen.

TUESDAY

WEEK I
LENTEN SEASON

PSALM 45 ▪ DEUTERONOMY 9:4-12 ▪ HEBREWS 3:1-11 ▪ JOHN 2:13-22

MORNING MEDITATIONS

PRAYER—Eternal and merciful Father, I give you humble thanks for all the spiritual and earthly blessings which in your mercy you have poured into my life. Lord, let me live only to love you and glorify your name. Amen. **JW**

PSALM 45:6-7a—Your throne, O God, endures forever and ever. Your royal scepter is a scepter of equity; you love righteousness and hate wickedness.

DEUTERONOMY 9:5   *God Keeps His Promises*
It is not because of your righteousness or the uprightness of your heart that you are going in to occupy their land; but because of the wickedness of these nations the LORD your God is dispossessing them before you, in order to fulfill the promise that the LORD made on oath to your ancestors.

HEBREWS 3:6-8a   *Do Not Harden Your Hearts*
Christ . . . was faithful over God's house as a son; and we are his house if we hold firm the confidence and the pride that belong to hope. Therefore, as the Holy Spirit says, "Today, if you hear his voice, do not harden your hearts."

JOHN 2:13-22   *Today's Gospel Reading*

From the Father through his Son, Jesus Christ, the Holy Spirit flows into us, and through the Holy Spirit . . . faith is given to us, and through faith Christ dwells in our hearts

FROM BONAVENTURE'S BREVILOQUIUM

EVENING REFLECTIONS

PSALM 48:9-10; 14—We ponder your steadfast love, O God, in the midst of your temple. Your name, O God, like your praise, reaches to the ends of the earth . . . our God will be our guide forever.

PRAYER—Come, Holy Spirit, fill the hearts of your people and kindle in us the fire of your love. Bring us rest and renewal through the quiet hours of the night, through Christ our Lord, I pray. Amen.

WEEK I ▪ LENTEN SEASON   27

PSALM 119:49-72 ▪ DEUTERONOMY 9:13-21 ▪ HEBREWS 3:12-19 ▪ JOHN 2:22—3:15

MORNING MEDITATIONS

PRAYER—Lord God, send your Holy Spirit to be the guide of all my ways and the sanctifier of my soul and body. Save, defend, and build me up in your love, through Christ my Lord. Amen. *JW*

PSALM 119:59-60—When I think of your ways, I turn my feet to your decrees; I hurry and do not delay to keep your commandments.

DEUTERONOMY 9:18 *The Lord Listened to Me*
Then I lay prostrate before the Lord as before, forty days and forty nights; I neither ate bread nor drank water, because of all the sin you had committed, provoking the Lord by doing what was evil in his sight.

HEBREWS 3:12-14 *Take Care*
Take care, brothers and sisters, that none of you may have an evil, unbelieving heart that turns away from the living God. But exhort one another every day . . . so that none of you may be hardened by the deceitfulness of sin. For we have become partners of Christ, if only we hold our first confidence firm to the end.

JOHN 2:22—3:15 *Today's Gospel Reading*

Christ is the Word of God; but the Word was made flesh. . . Therefore Christ is both victim and priest according to the spirit. For he who offers the sacrifice to his Father according to the flesh is himself offered upon the altar of the cross.

FROM ORIGEN'S HOMILIES ON GENESIS

EVENING REFLECTIONS

PSALM 49:7-8—Truly, no ransom avails for one's life, there is no price one can give to God for it. For the ransom of life is costly, and can never suffice.

PRAYER—Father, grant me forgiveness of what is past, that in the days to come I may with a pure spirit, do your will—walking humbly with you, showing love to all, and keeping body and soul in sanctification and honor, in Jesus' name. Amen. *JW*

PSALM 50 • DEUTERONOMY 9:23—10:5 • HEBREWS 4:1-11 • JOHN 3:16-21

MORNING MEDITATIONS

PRAYER—O Lord, I thank you for all your daily blessings, for keeping me through the night, and providing for my health, strength and comfort. May I always praise your holy name and love you, my Redeemer, in Jesus' name. Amen.

PSALM 50:1-2—The mighty one, God the LORD, speaks and summons the earth from the rising of the sun to its setting. Out of Zion, the perfection of beauty, God shines forth.

DEUTERONOMY 9:29 *God's Very Own Possession*
[These] are the people of your very own possession, whom you brought out by your great power and by your outstretched arm.

HEBREWS 4:9-11 *Rest in God*
So then, a sabbath rest still remains for the people of God; for those who enter God's rest also cease from their labors as God did from his. Let us therefore make every effort to enter that rest, so that none may fall through such disobedience.

JOHN 3:16-21 *Today's Gospel Reading*

Those who by God's gracious gift have become his children, born again from above of his Holy Spirit, possessing Christ within themselves to illuminate and recreate them, are guided in the many and varied ways of the Spirit as grace works in their hearts invisibly and in peace of soul.   FROM AN ANONYMOUS 4TH-CENTURY CHURCH THEOLOGIAN

EVENING REFLECTIONS

PSALM 46:4-5a, 10—There is a river whose streams make glad the city of God, the holy habitation of the Most High. God is in the midst of the city . . . Be still, and know that I am God!

PRAYER—My Lord and my God, you see my heart; and my desires are not hidden from you. I am encouraged and strengthened by your goodness to me today. I want to be yours and yours alone. O my God, my Savior, my Sanctifier, hear me, help me, and show mercy to me for Jesus Christ's sake. Amen. **JW**

PSALM 95 ▪ DEUTERONOMY 10:12-22 ▪ HEBREWS 4:12-16 ▪ JOHN 3:22-36

MORNING MEDITATIONS

PRAYER—God, come to my assistance; Lord, make haste to help me. Glory to the Father, and to the Son, and to the Holy Spirit; as it was in the beginning, is now, and will be forever. Amen.

PSALM 95:1, 3a, 7b—O come, let us sing to the LORD; let us make a joyful noise to the rock of our salvation! Let us come into his presence with thanksgiving . . . For the LORD is a great God . . . and we are the people of his pasture, and the sheep of his hand.

DEUTERONOMY 10:12-13a *The Essence of the Law*
What does the LORD your God require of you? Only to fear the LORD your God, to walk in all his ways, to love him, to serve the LORD your God with all your heart and with all your soul, and to keep the commandments of the LORD your God.

HEBREWS 4:12 *The Living Word*
The word of God is living and active, sharper than any two-edged sword, piercing until it divides soul from spirit, joints from marrow; it is able to judge the thoughts and intentions of the heart.

JOHN 3:22-36 *Today's Gospel Reading*

The Apostle says that he who by the Spirit puts to death the deeds of the body will live. Small wonder that he should live, since he who has the Spirit of God becomes a child of God.   AN EXCERPT FROM A LETTER OF ST. AMBROSE

EVENING REFLECTIONS

PSALM 51:1, 10—Have mercy on me, O God, according to your steadfast love; according to your abundant mercy blot out my transgressions . . . Create in me a clean heart, O God, and put a new and right spirit within me.

PRAYER—Father, accept my imperfect repentance, have compassion on my infirmities, forgive my faults, purify my uncleanness, strengthen my weakness, fix my unstableness, and let your good Spirit watch over me forever, and your love ever rule in my heart, through the merits and sufferings and love of your Son, in whom you are always well pleased. Amen. **JW**

PSALM 55 ▪ DEUTERONOMY 11:18-28 ▪ HEBREWS 5:1-10 ▪ JOHN 4:1-26

MORNING MEDITATIONS

PRAYER—Almighty God, to you all hearts are open, all desires known, and all secrets exposed; cleanse the thoughts of my heart by the inspiration of your Holy Spirit, that I may perfectly love you and worthily magnify your holy name, through Jesus Christ my Lord. Amen.

PSALM 55:16-17, 22—I call upon God, and the Lord will save me. Evening and morning and at noon I utter my complaint . . . and he will hear my voice . . . Cast your burden on the Lord, and he will sustain you; he will never permit the righteous to be moved.

DEUTERONOMY 11:18a, 19   *The Lord Listened to Me*
You shall put these words of mine in your heart and soul . . . teach them to your children, talking about them when you are at home and when you are away; when you lie down and when you rise.

HEBREWS 5:7-8   *He Learned Obedience*
In the days of his flesh, Jesus offered up prayers and supplications, with loud cries and tears, to the one who was able to save him from death, and he was heard because of his reverent submission. Although he was a Son, he learned obedience through what he suffered.

JOHN 4:1-26   *Today's Gospel Reading*

Now Christ is formed in a believer through faith implanted in his inmost soul. Such a one, gentle and lowly of heart, is summoned to the freedom of grace.
AN EXCERPT FROM AUGUSTINE'S EXPLANATION OF THE LETTER TO THE GALATIANS

EVENING REFLECTIONS

PSALM 138:3, 8—On the day I called, you answered me, you increased my strength of soul . . . the Lord will fulfill his purpose for me; your steadfast love, O Lord, endures forever.

PRAYER—Now to God the Father who first loved us, and made us accepted in the Beloved: to God the Son who loved us and washed us from our sins in his own blood; to God the Holy Spirit who fills our hearts with the love of God, be all love and all glory for time and for eternity. Amen. *JW*

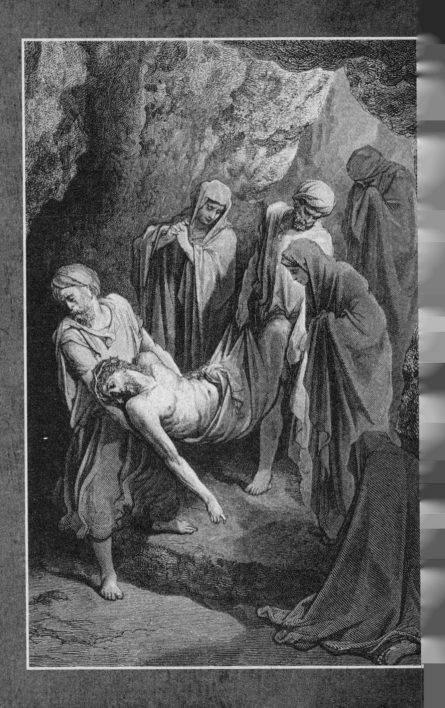

WEEK TWO
Lenten Season

Sunday: With Jesus After Dark

Read the Gospel passage from John 3:1-17, the devotional reflection titled "Wind of the Spirit," and then respond to the discussion prompts in the Reflective Journaling section.

THE MUSIC OF ASHES TO FIRE

Week 2: "God Who Saves" (Track 3)

Monday through Saturday of Week 2

IN THE MORNING:

A personal daily devotional guide includes prayer, a reading from the Old Testament, the Psalms, the Epistles, and the Gospel for each day of the week.

This week's readings are from Jeremiah, Romans, and the Gospel of John.

Inspirational quotes from men and women of faith keep us in contact with our shared Christian heritage.

IN THE EVENING:

An evening psalm and prayer become preludes to nighttime rest and renewal.

LENTEN SEASON—WEEK TWO
With Jesus After Dark

A devotional reflection based on John 3:1-17

Read the Gospel passage first, then the devotional reflection that follows. The discussion prompts at the end will help prepare you for Sunday school and small-group sessions.

Wind of the Spirit

The Pharisee and his servant, shouldering a heavy basket, made their way to the top of the mound of rock known as Skull Hill. Here was where imperial Rome executed criminals, rebels, and other disturbers of the empire. Today was no different, for jutting up from the craggy hill into the evening sky were three crosses, cruel instruments of Rome's iron rule.

As the hill climbers got closer, they could make out the details of the scene ahead. Two of the crosses held sagging, tortured bodies awaiting their removal by the Romans. No one had claimed their remains. The third cross in the middle held a lifeless man, battered beyond recognition. Gray and crusted with blood, he hung limply from the crosspiece. Leaning against the upright beam was a ladder, and already one of the man's good friends, Joseph, and his servants were removing the spikes from the man's hands and feet.

The Pharisee and his servant arrived just in time to help lower the body of the dead Nazarene Rabbi. Opening the basket, Nicodemus lifted out 75 pounds of myrrh and aloe, and he and Joseph of Arimathea, following Jewish custom, wrapped the body with linen, folding in the burial spices as they worked. When they had finished, they lifted the swaddled form onto a stretcher and, together with their servants, carried it to a newly cut tomb, provided by Joseph, in a nearby garden.

As he walked along in silence, holding the body of the dead Prophet, Nicodemus's emotions swirled with disappointment and sadness. Not long ago, as a member of the Sanhedrin, he had heard the command to the temple officers to arrest Jesus. But they had returned to the Sanhedrin, somehow unable to carry out their duty. When confronted with their failure, they could only respond, "No one ever spoke the way this man does."

Nicodemus thought about his own response to the charges against Jesus. He was glad now that he had defended him, although it had been risky. He had said, "Does our law condemn anyone without first hearing him to find out what he is doing?" The Sanhedrin had rebuked him then, and now they had succeeded in seizing Jesus—this One they accused of being a Messianic pretender. Overnight they had condemned him and the next day executed him. The words of the guards, "No one ever spoke the way this man does," called up another memory.

As he walked, Nicodemus remembered another night several months earlier. Like so many in Jerusalem, he had heard the rumors about Jesus, the popular Rabbi from Nazareth. Since almost everyone knew where Jesus lodged, Nicodemus had decided to seek him out. Passing through several dark alleyways he finally came to the home where Jesus was staying. After being received by the host, Nicodemus was soon face-to-face with the most confident, serene person he had ever met.

He remembered the first words he said to Jesus: "Rabbi, we know you are a teacher who has come from God, for no one could perform the miraculous signs you are doing if God were not with him."

Jesus had replied, "I tell you the truth. No one can see the kingdom of God unless he is born from above."

"How can a man be born when he is old?" He caught himself speaking the words aloud, as though he were conversing again with the One whose body he was now carrying. "Surely he cannot enter a second time into his mother's womb to be born."

With a gentle smile Jesus then said, "I tell you the truth no one can enter the kingdom of God unless he is born of water and the Spirit. Flesh gives birth to flesh, but the Spirit gives birth to spirit." Just then a breeze from the west off the Great Sea reached them, bringing relief to the sultry summer night. Jesus noticed. He was always aware of the natural world around him.

"You should not be surprised at my saying you must be born from above. The wind blows wherever it pleases. You hear its sound, but you cannot tell where it comes from or where it is going. So it is with everyone born of the Spirit."

That night, as Nicodemus had asked, "How can this be?" an unpredictable, unexpected breath from God, like a gentle breeze from heaven, began to blow across the landscape of his tired, lean spirit, and something miraculous began to happen deep within him.

✝✝✝

Like many people, Nicodemus had wanted his religious life to be predictable, controllable, and clearly regulated with precisely ordered spiritual laws. But that was before everything changed. That was before he met Jesus.

When this Nazarene Rabbi came along with his word pictures about things that are uncontrollable—like wind, which comes and goes and swirls and goes again or like birth from above, from the top down—suddenly something happened. Nicodemus experienced a new everlasting and liberating way of life. Jesus opened the window to the confining, overly regulated life of legality and released Nicodemus to new vistas of living.

This is the freedom Jesus offers all of us when he says, "God so loved the world that he gave his only Son, so that everyone who believes in him may not perish but may have eternal life" (John 3:16).

✝✝✝

Nicodemus looked down at the dead Rabbi. He saw death but was experiencing life. Something from above was happening down inside. He mused about where this might lead him. He didn't know. Perhaps his ancestor Abraham had felt like this when he had set off from Ur for places unknown. Just then a soft wind blew through the garden, bringing with it the warm, hopeful aromas of spring's first blooms. He looked back and noticed the simple T-shaped cross against the red evening sky. The sight stirred him with life-giving images: "As Moses lifted up the serpent in the wilderness, so must the Son of Man be lifted up, that whoever believes in him may have eternal life" (vv. 14-15).

Nicodemus savored the moment like a child fascinated with some new discovery. Then together with his friend Joseph, he stooped through the opening of the burial cave, carried the body of Jesus inside to its resting place, and gently laid it on a stone shelf. As he turned to leave, his heart echoed with words that were changing his life: "Everyone who believes . . . [will] not perish but . . . have eternal life" (v. 16). —MN

After reading the passage from John 3 and the devotional reflection "Wind of the Spirit," you may also want to read the following related passages:

Genesis 12:1-4a; Psalm 121; and Romans 4:1-5, 13-17

The **discussion prompts** that follow will help prepare you to participate in your Sunday school class or small-group study. Use your **reflective journaling** section to record any other insights that come to you as you read the Gospel lesson and the devotional reflection.

DISCUSSION PROMPT #1: JOHN 3

In what ways does Nicodemus' literal understanding of birth keep him from understanding what Jesus is offering? How does Jesus' understanding of "born from above" differ from physical birth or simply "turning over a new leaf"?

DISCUSSION PROMPT #2: JOHN 3

Read verse 12 again. Does Jesus mean we can never understand this new life? Why? Would the answer change if we added "fully understand" to the question? Why?

DISCUSSION PROMPT #3: JOHN 3

Does eternal life relate only to that period after we die? Why?

DISCUSSION PROMPT #4: DEVOTIONAL REFLECTION

How does the devotional reflection add to your understanding of this encounter between Jesus and Nicodemus?

REFLECTIVE JOURNALING

_____

_____

_____

_____

_____

_____

_____

_____

_____

_____

_____

_____

_____

_____

_____

_____

_____

_____

_____

_____

_____

_____

_____

_____

_____

_____

_____

_____

_____

_____

_____

PSALM 56 ▪ JEREMIAH 1:1-19 ▪ ROMANS 1:1-15 ▪ JOHN 4:27-42

MORNING MEDITATIONS

PRAYER—O God, you are the giver of all good gifts and I desire to praise your name for all of your goodness to me. I thank you for sending your Son to die for my sins, for the means of grace, and for the hope of glory, through Jesus Christ. Amen. *JW*

PSALM 56:2b-4a—O Most High, when I am afraid, I put my trust in you. In God, whose word I praise, in God I trust; I am not afraid.

JEREMIAH 1:4, 7b *I Appointed You*
Now the word of the LORD came to me saying, "Before I formed you in the womb I knew you, and before you were born I consecrated you; I appointed you a prophet . . . for you shall go to all to whom I send you, and you shall speak whatever I command you."

ROMANS 1:1, 3-4 *Servant of Christ*
Paul, a servant of Jesus Christ . . . who was descended from David according to the flesh and was declared to be Son of God with power according to the spirit of holiness by resurrection from the dead, Jesus Christ our Lord.

JOHN 4:27-42 *Today's Gospel Reading*

Many listen more willingly to the world than to God and are readier to follow the desires of their flesh than God's good pleasure . . . Jesus is the rewarder of all the good, and the mighty power of all the devout.

AN EXCERPT FROM *THE IMITATION OF CHRIST* BY THOMAS À KEMPIS

EVENING REFLECTIONS

PSALM 65:1, 5—Praise is due to you, O God, in Zion; and to you shall vows be performed . . . By awesome deeds you answer us with deliverance, O God of our salvation; you are the hope of all the ends of the earth.

PRAYER (PSALM 51:17, 7)—O Lord, "the sacrifice acceptable [to you] is a broken spirit; a broken and contrite heart, O God, you will not despise . . . Purge me with hyssop, and I shall be clean; wash me, and I shall be whiter than snow." Amen.

PSALM 61 ▪ JEREMIAH 2:1-13 ▪ ROMANS 1:16-25 ▪ JOHN 4:43-54

MORNING MEDITATIONS

PRAYER—Blessed are you, Sovereign God of all, to you be praise and glory forever. Open our eyes to behold your presence and strengthen our hands to do your will, that the world may rejoice and give you praise. Amen.

PSALM 61:1-3—Hear my cry, O God; listen to my prayer . . . Lead me to the rock that is higher than I; for you are my refuge, a strong tower against the enemy.

JEREMIAH 2:12-13 *Empty Cisterns*
Be appalled, O heavens, at this, be shocked . . . says the Lord, for my people have committed two evils: they have forsaken me, the fountain of living water, and dug out cracked cisterns for themselves . . . that can hold no water.

ROMANS 1:16-17 *The Power of the Gospel*
I am not ashamed of the gospel; it is the power of God for salvation to everyone who has faith . . . for in it the righteousness of God is revealed through faith for faith; as it is written, "The one who is righteous will live by faith."

JOHN 4:43-54 *Today's Gospel Reading*

When our Lord Jesus Christ, while never ceasing to be true God, was born true man, he himself became the prelude of a new creation, and in the manner of his coming he gave the human race a spiritual beginning.   AN EXCERPT FROM A SERMON BY LEO THE GREAT

EVENING REFLECTIONS

PSALM 68:19-20a, 35b—Blessed be the Lord, who daily bears us up; God is our salvation. Our God is a God of salvation . . . he gives power and strength to his people.

PRAYER (PSALM 51:17, 10)—O Lord, "the sacrifice acceptable [to you] is a broken spirit; a broken and contrite heart, O God, you will not despise . . . Create in me a clean heart, O God, and put a new and right spirit within me." Amen.

PSALM 72 ▪ JEREMIAH 3:6-18 ▪ ROMANS 1:28—2:11 ▪ JOHN 5:1-18

MORNING MEDITATIONS

PRAYER—Lord God, send your Holy Spirit to be the guide of all my ways and the sanctifier of my soul and body. Give me the light of your presence, your peace from heaven, and the salvation of my soul, through Jesus Christ my Lord. Amen. **JW**

PSALM 72:18-19—Blessed be the Lord, the God of Israel, who alone does wondrous things. Blessed be his glorious name forever; may his glory fill the whole earth. Amen.

JEREMIAH 3:12-13a, 14   *The Lord Is Merciful*
I will not look on you in anger, for I am merciful, says the Lord; I will not be angry forever. Only acknowledge your guilt, that you have rebelled against the Lord your God . . . Return, O faithless children, says the Lord . . . and I will bring you to Zion.

ROMANS 2:4b, 9-10   *God's Kindness Leads to Repentance*
Do you not realize that God's kindness is meant to lead you to repentance? . . . There will be anguish and distress for everyone who does evil . . . but glory and honor and peace for everyone who does good.

JOHN 5:1-18   *Today's Gospel Reading*

> Of old we were poisoned by a tree; now we have found immortality through a tree. Of old we were led astray by a tree; now we have repelled the treacherous snake by means of a tree. Indeed an unheard-of exchange! We are given life instead of death, incorruptibility instead of corruption, glory instead of dishonor.
>
> A READING FROM *ON THE ADORATION OF THE CROSS*, ST. THEODORE, THE STUDITE

EVENING REFLECTIONS

PSALM 119:80-81—May my heart be blameless in your statutes, so that I may not be put to shame. My soul languishes for your salvation; I hope in your word.

PRAYER (PSALM 51:17, 12)—O Lord, "the sacrifice acceptable [to you] is a broken spirit; a broken and contrite heart, O God, you will not despise . . . Restore to me the joy of your salvation, and sustain in me a willing spirit." Amen.

PSALM 71 ▪ JEREMIAH 4:9-14, 19-28 ▪ ROMANS 2:12-24 ▪ JOHN 5:19-29

MORNING MEDITATIONS

PRAYER—O Eternal God, my Savior and Lord, I acknowledge that all I am and all I have is yours. I pray that you will surround me with such a sense of your infinite goodness, that I may return to you all possible love and obedience, through Jesus Christ, Amen. *JW*

PSALM 71:1-2—In you, O LORD, I take refuge; let me never be put to shame. In your righteousness deliver me and rescue me; incline your ear to me and save me.

JEREMIAH 4:14   *The Lord Listened to Me*
O Jerusalem, wash your heart clean of wickedness so that you may be saved.

ROMANS 2:12-13   *Do What Is Right*
All who have sinned apart from the law will also perish apart from the law, and all who have sinned under the law will be judged by the law. For it is not the hearers of the law who are righteous in God's sight, but the doers of the law who will be justified.

JOHN 5:19-29   *Today's Gospel Reading*

Worship in the Spirit . . . is carried on, as it were, in the light, as may be learned from the words spoken to the woman of Samaria. She was misled to believe that God was worshipped in a place. Our Lord corrected her; he said that we must worship in Spirit and in truth, and by "truth" he clearly meant himself.
A READING FROM THE TREATISE, *ON THE HOLY SPIRIT* BY ST. BASIL THE GREAT

EVENING REFLECTIONS

PSALM 74:12, 20-22a—Yet God my King is from old, working salvation in the earth . . . Have regard for your covenant, for the dark places of the land are full of the haunts of violence. Do not let the downtrodden be put to shame; let the poor and needy praise your name. Rise up, O God, plead your cause.

PRAYER (PSALM 51:17, 6)—O Lord, "the sacrifice acceptable [to you] is a broken spirit; a broken and contrite heart, O God, you will not despise . . . You desire truth in the inward being; therefore teach me wisdom in my secret heart." Amen.

FRIDAY

PSALM 69 • JEREMIAH 5:1-9 • ROMANS 2:25—3:18 • JOHN 5:30-47

MORNING MEDITATIONS

PRAYER—Holy God, in your compassion and mercy, your light breaks forth in our darkness and your healing springs up for our deliverance. Sustain us with your bountiful Spirit as we rejoice in your saving help, in the name of Christ, I pray. Amen.

PSALM 69:13, 18—My prayer is to you, O LORD. At an acceptable time, O God, in the abundance of your steadfast love, answer me . . . Draw near to me, redeem me, set me free.

JEREMIAH 5:3 *God Looks for Truth*
O LORD, do your eyes not look for truth? You have struck [the untruthful], but they felt no anguish; you have consumed them, but they refused to take correction.

ROMANS 3:10, 18 *No One Is Righteous*
There is no one who is righteous, not even one; there is no one who has understanding, there is no one who seeks God . . . there is no fear of God before their eyes.

JOHN 5:30-47 *Today's Gospel Reading*

Out of the abundance of his love, without grudging, God adopted us as his children, and granted that we might know God as Father and love him with all our hearts, and follow his Word without turning aside.   A READING FROM *AGAINST THE HERESIES* BY IRENAEUS

EVENING REFLECTIONS

PSALM 73:25-26—Whom have I in heaven but you? And there is nothing on earth that I desire other than you. My flesh and my heart may fail, but God is the strength of my heart and my portion forever.

PRAYER (PSALM 51:17, 11)—O Lord, "the sacrifice acceptable [to you] is a broken spirit; a broken and contrite heart, O God, you will not despise . . . Do not cast me away from your presence, and do not take your holy spirit from me." Amen.

PSALM 75 ▪ JEREMIAH 5:20-31 ▪ ROMANS 3:19-31 ▪ JOHN 7:1-13

MORNING MEDITATIONS

PRAYER—Blessed are you, Sovereign God, ruler and judge of all. In the darkness of this age that is passing away, may the glory of your kingdom surround our steps as we journey on our way, in the name of Christ, I pray. Amen.

PSALM 75:1-2, 7—We give thanks to you, O God; we give thanks; your name is near. People tell of your wondrous deeds. At the set time that [you] appoint [you] will judge with equity . . . it is God who executes judgment, putting down one and lifting up another.

JEREMIAH 5:24a-25   *Sin Deprives Us of Good*
They do not say in their hearts, "Let us fear the LORD our God, who gives the rain in its season . . . and keeps for us the weeks . . . of harvest." Your iniquities have turned these away, and your sins have deprived you of good.

ROMANS 3:21b-24   *All Have Sinned*
The righteousness of God has been disclosed . . . for all who believe. For there is no distinction, since all have sinned and fall short of the glory of God; they are now justified by his grace as a gift, through the redemption that is in Christ Jesus.

JOHN 7:1-13   *Today's Gospel Reading*

Because God is good and especially good to those who serve him, we must cling to him, and be with him with all our soul and with all our heart and with all our strength. This we must do if we are to live in his light.

A READING FROM *ON FLIGHT FROM THE WORLD,* BY ST. AMBROSE

EVENING REFLECTIONS

PSALM 27:1—The LORD is my light and my salvation; whom shall I fear? The LORD is the stronghold of my life; of whom shall I be afraid?

PRAYER (PSALM 51:17, 7)—O Lord, "the sacrifice acceptable [to you] is a broken spirit; a broken and contrite heart, O God, you will not despise . . . Purge me with hyssop, and I shall be clean; wash me, and I shall be whiter than snow." Amen.

WEEK THREE
LENTEN SEASON

Sunday: With Jesus at a Well

Read the Gospel passage from John 4:4-24, the devotional reflection titled "Honest to God," and respond to the discussion prompts in the Reflective Journaling section.

THE MUSIC OF ASHES TO FIRE

Week 3: "Send the Water" (Track 4)

Monday through Saturday of Week 3

IN THE MORNING:

A personal daily devotional guide includes prayer, a reading from the Old Testament, the Psalms, the Epistles, and the Gospel for each day of the week.

This week's readings are from Jeremiah, Romans, and the Gospel of John.

Inspirational quotes from men and women of faith keep us in contact with our shared Christian heritage.

IN THE EVENING:

An evening psalm and prayer become preludes to nighttime rest and renewal.

LENTEN SEASON–WEEK THREE
With Jesus at a Well

A devotional reflection based on John 4:4-24

Read the Gospel passage first, then the devotional reflection that follows. The discussion prompts at the end will help prepare you for Sunday school and small-group sessions.

Honest to God

HOW JESUS TALKS TO PEOPLE WHO DON'T "BELONG"

The preachers of my childhood loved to scare me to death. They sometimes painted vivid images of what things would be like at the end of the world. Some preachers told us that we had better be good because at the final day when we all stand before God to give account for our lives, here's what we could expect.

A giant video screen would appear over the throne of God. Displayed on that screen for all the world to see would be not only everything we ever did but also everything we ever thought about doing! It was an effective tool, at least for getting us to come forward to the altar. I'm not sure how effective it was in really changing our behavior, but who wouldn't be mortified at the thought? If people knew everything about us, we would be horrified, embarrassed, ashamed.

The truth is, millions of people in this world go about in virtual hiding. People are afraid to let anybody get close to them because they think if folks knew, if they really knew who they are or what they have done, they would be despised.

The Gospel of John gives us a wonderful snapshot into the life of Jesus that provides a picture much different from what some of my childhood preachers gave of who God is and how God treats those whose lives have been wrecked by failure and sin. This story is about how God comes to people who do not think they belong.

Jesus and his friends were traveling north from the area around Jerusalem up to Galilee, which is where they spent most of their time. John says that Jesus "had to go through Samaria." Well, not really. Actually, Jewish travelers on this route regularly avoided Samaria, taking a longer route. Why? This was about a division and mistrust that went back hundreds of years. We hear the Jewish attitude about Samaritans in John's comment: *"for Jews do not associate with Samaritans."* So there!

No, Jesus didn't have to be here, he *chose* to be here. He is here to confront prejudice and break down walls. He is here to heal wounds and divisions. It's the middle of the day, and Jesus is tired and thirsty. The trip brings him through the town of Sychar, where Jacob's well is located. Jesus sends his companions off to buy groceries while he sits by the well with his eyes and heart opened, watching for souls who have decided they are outside the interest of God.

That's when she comes. She didn't come in the morning or late in the day as the other women; she comes alone in the middle of the day. It hints at her position in the community—outcast. Jesus violates all social custom by asking her for a drink of water. She is taken a back, as will be everyone who hears about this. It's just not normal, nearly scandalous.

Jesus says something about living water. It does not seem to be a great conversation starter, but he sees something in her that we do not see. He can see that this woman is in hiding. She's afraid, so she dodges his questions and tries to change the subject. So what does Jesus do? He lets her know that he knows. "Go call your husband."

"I don't have a husband," is her veiled reply.

"That's true. In fact, you've gone through five husbands and you're living with somebody now who is not your husband."

Oh no, her worst fear is realized—that somebody will know all about her. Jesus has her undivided attention!

She responds nervously, "Sir, I perceive that you are a prophet." No kidding!

With one master stroke Jesus opens the woman's deepest self. But here's the difference: Jesus doesn't do it to be harsh or cruel. He simply knows that if she cannot face herself and admit that her tangled relationships are sin, she can never drink of living water. The gift is free, but it cannot be received without honest self-disclosure.

She wants to change the subject—and fast! She brings up an old controversy about where the proper place for worship really is. This is just like us, isn't it?

Anytime Jesus starts to get too close, we want to bring up all kinds of other issues to keep the spotlight off our real selves. Jesus is not deterred, though, because of his love. Now that the woman's pain and history has been revealed, now that she's had to admit it, Jesus cuts right to the heart of the issue.

"True worshipers will worship the Father in spirit and truth." What does he mean? Jesus is talking about nothing more and nothing less than honest self-disclosure. This is about being real. It is about becoming honest with myself and honest with God about who I really am.

What changes this woman and eventually will change her entire hometown is that even though Jesus peered into the ugly truth of her life, he did not push her away and did not rule her out. He accepted her and that's why her testimony becomes, "Come and see a man who told me everything I ever did. Could this be the Christ?"

Do you hear what I hear behind those words? Come and see a man who knows everything about me and still loves me. Come and see a man who watched the video screen of my life and yet did not push me away. Could it be, is it possible that this is the Christ? In other words, could this be a picture of who God really is?

This woman had a lot of defensiveness. She was defensive about many things because she had a lot to hide. She believed the judgment of her community that she was not worthy of love. She was waiting for a messenger from God who would come with good news that the arms of God are opened in love to forgive, heal, and make new. And one day she met a man, a God-Man, who said to her, "I who speak to you am he."

Jesus came for this purpose. Jesus came to show us that we can come out of hiding. Jesus came to show us that the Father invites us to come into the full light of the truth, not to be ashamed and embarrassed, but to be forgiven and restored. The truth is that if we will open ourselves up to Jesus and be honest to God, that's when we begin to drink from his living water. That's when we become real. —JR

After reading the passage from John 4 and the
devotional reflection "Honest to God," you may also
want to read the following related passages:
Exodus 17:1-7; Psalm 95; Romans 5:1-11

The **discussion prompts** that follow will help prepare you to participate in your Sunday school class or small-group study. Use your **reflective journaling** section to record any other insights that come to you as you read the Gospel lesson and the devotional reflection.

DISCUSSION PROMPT #1: JOHN 4

Jesus and the Samaritan woman spoke the same language, but in what ways did they "talk past each other" in their conversation?

DISCUSSION PROMPT #2: JOHN 4

In what ways are we responsible for good communication in our conversation with others?

DISCUSSION PROMPT #3: JOHN 4

Was what Jesus knew about the woman's life the same thing as judging her? Why or why not?

DISCUSSION PROMPT #4: DEVOTIONAL REFLECTION

What social conventions or taboos were broken in this story? Why do you think they are important to this passage?

DISCUSSION PROMPT #5: JOHN 4

How was the townspeople's first-hand experience of Jesus more effective for their conversion than merely hearing about him? What does that say about our own lives? Why?

REFLECTIVE JOURNALING

_____

_____

_____

_____

_____

_____

_____

_____

PSALM 80 ▪ JEREMIAH 7:1-15 ▪ ROMANS 4:1-12 ▪ JOHN 7:14-36

MORNING MEDITATIONS

PRAYER (BCP)—Our Father in heaven, hallowed be your Name,
your kingdom come, your will be done, on earth as in heaven.
Give us today our daily bread.
Forgive us our sins as we forgive those who sin against us.
Save us from the time of trial, and deliver us from evil.
For the kingdom, the power, and the glory are yours, now and for
ever. Amen.

PSALM 80:14, 18b-19—Turn again, O God of hosts; look down from heaven, and see
. . . give us life, and we will call on your name. Restore us, O Lord God of hosts; let your face
shine, that we may be saved.

JEREMIAH 7:5-7a *Amend Your Ways*
If you truly amend your ways and your doings, if you truly act justly one with another, if you
do not oppress the alien, the orphan and the widow or . . . go after other gods, . . . then I
will dwell with you in this place.

ROMANS 4:6-7 *Faith Reckoned as Righteousness*
David speaks of the blessedness of those to whom God reckons righteousness apart from
works: "Blessed are those whose iniquities are forgiven, and whose sins are covered."

JOHN 7:14-36 *Today's Gospel Reading*

Paul boasts of the fact that he despises his own righteousness, but seeks that righteousness by faith which comes through Christ, which comes from God . . . Here all the
loftiness of pride has fallen. Nothing of which we may boast is left, living totally in the
grace and free gift of God.   AN EXCERPT FROM *HOMILY 20* BY BASIL THE GREAT

EVENING REFLECTIONS

PSALM 77:11-12, 14a—I will call to mind the deeds of the Lord; I will remember your
wonders of old. I will meditate on all your work, and muse on your might deeds . . . You are
the God who works wonders.

PRAYER—O God, fill my soul with so entire a love for you, that I may love nothing but
you. Give me grace to study your knowledge daily, that the more I know you, the more I
may love you, through Jesus Christ my Lord. Amen. **JW**

PSALM 78 ▪ JEREMIAH 7:21-34 ▪ ROMANS 4:13-25 ▪ JOHN 7:37-52

MORNING MEDITATIONS

PRAYER (BCP)—Our Father in heaven, hallowed be your Name,
your kingdom come, your will be done, on earth as in heaven.
Give us today our daily bread.
Forgive us our sins as we forgive those who sin against us.
Save us from the time of trial, and deliver us from evil.
For the kingdom, the power, and the glory are yours, now and for
ever. Amen.

PSALM 78:1, 4—Give ear, O my people, to my teaching; incline your ears to the words of my mouth . . . we will tell to the coming generation the glorious deeds of the Lᴏʀᴅ and his might, and the wonders he has done.

JEREMIAH 7:22b, 23   *Obey My Voice*
I did not command . . . [your ancestors] concerning burnt offerings . . . But this command I gave them, "Obey my voice, and I will be your God, and you shall be my people; and walk in the way that I command you, so that it may be well with you."

ROMANS 4:20-21   *Fully Convinced*
No distrust made [Abraham] waver concerning the promise of God, but he grew strong in his faith as he gave glory to God, being fully convinced that God was able to do what he had promised.

JOHN 7:37-52   *Today's Gospel Reading*

When the word is preached . . . it gives to its own voice which is heard outwardly, a voice inwardly sensed . . . by which the dead live again, and from the stones are raised up children to Abraham.   A PORTION FROM *TREATISE 6* BY BALDWIN OF CANTERBURY

EVENING REFLECTIONS

PSALM 78:1a, 5b-7a—Give ear, O my people, to my teaching . . . He commanded our ancestors to teach their children; that the next generation might know . . . and rise up and tell them to their children, so that they should set their hope in God.

PRAYER—O Lamb of God, in this evening sacrifice of praise and prayer, I offer you a contrite heart. Give me grace, throughout my whole life, in every thought, and word, and work to imitate your meekness and humility, through Christ, my Lord, I pray. Amen. *JW*

PSALM 119:97-120 ▪ JEREMIAH 8:18—9:6 ▪ ROMANS 5:1-11 ▪ JOHN 8:12-20

MORNING MEDITATIONS

PRAYER (BCP)—Our Father in heaven, hallowed be your Name,
your kingdom come, your will be done, on earth as in heaven.
Give us today our daily bread.
Forgive us our sins as we forgive those who sin against us.
Save us from the time of trial, and deliver us from evil.
For the kingdom, the power, and the glory are yours, now and for
ever. Amen.

PSALM 119:97-98, 105—Oh, how I love your law! It is my meditation all day long.
Your commandment makes me wiser than my enemies, for it is always with me . . . Your
word is a lamp to my feet and a light to my path.

JEREMIAH 8:20, 22; 9:1 *There Is a Balm in Gilead*
"The harvest is past, the summer is ended, and we are not saved." . . . Is there no balm in
Gilead? Is there no physician there? . . . O that my eyes were a fountain of tears so that I
might weep day and night for . . . my poor people.

ROMANS 5:8 *God Loves Us*
But God proves his love for us in that while we still were sinners Christ died for us.

JOHN 8:12-20 *Today's Gospel Reading*

If you will you can be cured. Deliver yourself to the physician, and he will cure the eyes of
your soul and heart. Who is the physician? He is God, who heals and gives life through his
Word.   AN EXCERPT FROM A BOOK OF THEOPHILUS OF ANTIOCH

EVENING REFLECTIONS

PSALM 81:10a, 13, 16—I am the LORD your God . . . O that my people would listen to
me, that [they] would walk in my ways! . . . I would feed you with the finest of wheat, and
with honey from the rock I would satisfy you.

PRAYER—O Lord, whose whole life cried out, "Father, not my will, but your will be done,"
give me grace to walk after your pattern and to follow in your steps. Give me grace to take
up my cross, in Jesus' name. Amen. *JW*

PSALM 42 ▪ JEREMIAH 10:11-24 ▪ ROMANS 5:12-21 ▪ JOHN 8:21-32

MORNING MEDITATIONS

PRAYER (BCP)—Our Father in heaven, hallowed be your Name,
your kingdom come, your will be done, on earth as in heaven.
Give us today our daily bread.
Forgive us our sins as we forgive those who sin against us.
Save us from the time of trial, and deliver us from evil.
For the kingdom, the power, and the glory are yours, now and for
ever. Amen.

PSALM 42:1, 11—As a deer longs for flowing streams, so my soul longs for you, O God
. . . Why are you cast down, O my soul, and why are you disquieted within me? Hope in
God; for I shall again praise him, my help and my God.

JEREMIAH 10:12, 16b   *The Lord of Hosts Is His Name*
It is he who made the earth by his power, who established the world by his wisdom, and by
his understanding stretched out the heavens . . . the LORD of hosts is his name.

ROMANS 5:20-21   *Abounding Grace*
Where sin increased, grace abounded all the more, so that, just as sin exercised dominion
in death, so grace might also exercise dominion through justification leading to eternal life
through Jesus Christ our Lord.

JOHN 8:21-32   *Today's Gospel Reading*

Prayer is the offering which he has asked for, and which he has provided for himself. This
is the sacrifice, offered from the heart, fed on faith, prepared by truth, unblemished in
innocence, pure in chastity, and garlanded with love which we must bring to God's altar.

FROM THE TREATISE OF TERTULLIAN ON PRAYER

EVENING REFLECTIONS

PSALM 85:10-11—Steadfast love and faithfulness will meet; righteousness and peace
will kiss each other. Faithfulness will spring up from the ground, and righteousness will look
down from the sky.

PRAYER—My Lord and my God, you see my heart; and my desires are not hidden from
you. I am encouraged and strengthened by your goodness to me today. I want to be yours
and yours alone. O my God, my Savior, my Sanctifier, hear me, help me, and show mercy to
me for Jesus Christ's sake. Amen. ***JW***

PSALM 88 ▪ JEREMIAH 11:1-8 ▪ ROMANS 6:1-11 ▪ JOHN 8:33-47

MORNING MEDITATIONS

PRAYER (BCP)—Our Father in heaven, hallowed be your Name,
your kingdom come, your will be done, on earth as in heaven.
Give us today our daily bread.
Forgive us our sins as we forgive those who sin against us.
Save us from the time of trial, and deliver us from evil.
For the kingdom, the power, and the glory are yours, now and for
ever. Amen.

PSALM 88:13, 9b—But I, O LORD, cry out to you; in the morning my prayer comes
before you. . . . Every day I call on you, O LORD; I spread out my hands to you.

JEREMIAH 11:3b, 4b   Listen
Thus says the LORD, the God of Israel: Cursed be anyone who does not heed the words of
this covenant . . . Listen to my voice, and do all that I command you. So shall you be my
people, and I will be your God.

ROMANS 6:1-2, 6   Crucified with Christ
What then are we to say? Should we continue in sin in order that grace may abound? By no
means! How can we who died to sin go on living in it? . . . We know that our old self was
crucified with him so that the body of sin might be destroyed.

JOHN 8:33-47   Today's Gospel Reading

Just as the physical body of Christ was nailed to the cross and buried and afterwards
raised to life, so the whole body of Christ's saints has been nailed to the cross with Christ
. . . We have been buried therefore with Christ and we have risen with him.

FROM THE COMMENTARY OF ORIGEN ON THE GOSPEL OF JOHN

EVENING REFLECTIONS

PSALM 88:1-2—O LORD, God of my salvation, when, at night, I cry out in your presence,
let my prayer come before you; incline your ear to my cry.

PRAYER—Father, accept my imperfect repentance, have compassion on my infirmities,
forgive my faults, purify my uncleanness, strengthen my weakness, fix my unstableness, and
let your good Spirit watch over me forever, and your love ever rule in my heart, through the
merits and sufferings and love of your Son, in whom you are always well pleased. Amen. **JW**

*S*ATURDAY

WEEK 3
LENTEN SEASON

PSALM 90 ▪ JEREMIAH 13:1-17 ▪ ROMANS 6:12-23 ▪ JOHN 8:47-59

MORNING MEDITATIONS

PRAYER (BCP)—Our Father in heaven, hallowed be your Name,
your kingdom come, your will be done, on earth as in heaven.
Give us today our daily bread.
Forgive us our sins as we forgive those who sin against us.
Save us from the time of trial, and deliver us from evil.
For the kingdom, the power, and the glory are yours, now and for ever. Amen.

PSALM 90:1-2—Lord, you have been our dwelling place in all generations. Before the mountains were brought forth, or ever you had formed the earth and the world, from everlasting to everlasting you are God.

JEREMIAH 13:15-16a, 17a   *Do Not Be Haughty*
Hear and give ear; do not be haughty, for the LORD has spoken. Give glory to the LORD your God before he brings darkness, and before your feet stumble on the mountains . . . If you will not listen, my soul will weep in secret for your pride.

ROMANS 6:22-23   *The Free Gift of God*
But now that you have been freed from sin and enslaved to God, the advantage you get is sanctification. The end is eternal life. For the wages of sin is death, but the free gift of God is eternal life in Christ Jesus our Lord.

JOHN 8:47-59   *Today's Gospel Reading*

Man desires to praise you. He is but a tiny part of all that you have created. He bears about him his mortality . . . yet this tiny part of all that you have created desires to praise you . . . For you have made us for yourself and our hearts are restless till they rest in you.

AN EXCERPT FROM *THE CONFESSIONS* OF ST. AUGUSTINE

EVENING REFLECTIONS

PSALM 90:17—Let the favor of the Lord our God be upon us, and prosper for us the work of our hands—O prosper the work of our hands!

PRAYER—All the powers of my soul are too few to compose the thankful praise that is due to you. Yet you have declared that you will accept the sacrifice of thanksgiving, in return for all your goodness. Therefore, I will bless you, adore your power, and magnify your holy Name. Amen. *JW*

WEEK 3 ▪ LENTEN SEASON   59

WEEK FOUR
Lenten Season

Sunday: With Jesus Along the Road

Read the Gospel passage from John 9:1-41, the devotional reflection titled "Blind, but Now I See!" and respond to the discussion prompts in the Reflective Journaling section.

THE MUSIC OF ASHES TO FIRE

Week 4: "Love's Already Won" (Track 5)

Monday through Saturday of Week 4

IN THE MORNING:

A personal daily devotional guide includes prayer, a reading from the Old Testament, the Psalms, the Epistles, and the Gospel for each day of the week.

This week's readings are from Jeremiah, Romans, and the Gospel of John.

Inspirational quotes from men and women of faith keep us in contact with our shared Christian heritage.

IN THE EVENING:

An evening psalm and prayer become preludes to nighttime rest and renewal.

*L*ENTEN *S*EASON–WEEK FOUR
With Jesus Along the Road

A devotional reflection based on John 9:1-41

*R*ead the Gospel passage first, then the devotional reflection that follows. The discussion prompts at the end will help prepare you for Sunday school and small-group sessions.

Blind, but Now I See!

Jesus sees.

It's a simple fact. Jesus sees you. But Jesus sees you in a different light. He sees you in the full light of truth. He is not blinded by pretense or assumption. He knows our exact condition. He understands our specific situation. He sees our inability to see.

I was sitting in the bookstore when I noticed the man in a powered wheelchair. He had an obvious disability and was unable to fully move his arms and legs. As he stopped his wheelchair near where I was sitting, he stared upward, appearing to want a closer look at a book on one of the upper shelves. I spoke to him: "Would you like me to get something down for you?"

At first, I wondered if he had even heard my question. But after a few seconds, he slowly turned his wheelchair toward me and coldly stared at me for a moment before stating in a firm voice, "If I needed your help, I would have asked for it."

I was stunned. My gesture of kindness had been thoroughly rejected. Sometimes the way people see injustice affects the way they respond to help. Maybe the man thought the injustice in his life was in some way his fault and that he didn't want or deserve help. After all, if he believed he caused it, he could easily reason that only he should deal with the consequences. This way of looking at injustice is not new. In John 9 the disciples were thinking along the same lines about the man born blind.

Like many people in their day, the disciples believed that the man was blind because of sin. They assumed life was fair, with their good or bad actions (or even their parents' actions) always yielding equal consequences. In a way, they believed they were upholding God's justice by declaring that some things in life only *seem* to be unfair. But this assumption was based on the false idea that the world operates through karma, that actions decide destiny.

We still desire to make this form of justice work in our lives today. Though we have healthy theologies that try to correct our subconscious thinking, we still silently struggle with the notion that "everything happens for a reason" and that *we* are the cause of the injustices in our lives.

Like the disciples, we are as blind to truth as the blind man was to light. We share this common temptation to quickly connect injustice and sin. We often live with a self-imposed scar that whatever injustices we suffer, we supposedly deserve them. We quickly convince ourselves when things go wrong that we are somehow being punished for our actions. We try to muster up belief within ourselves that injustice *must* be fair, that our wrongs must deserve God's punishment in this way.

Then Jesus speaks.

Being born blind doesn't mean you or your parents have sinned. Your heartache doesn't mean God is punishing you. You are not the living consequence of poor choices. And even when everyone around you assumes your injustices are self-imposed, Jesus sees the truth about you.

Life isn't always fair. Our actions will always have consequences, but not all consequences are equal to the actions. Kindness is not always returned with gratitude. And sometimes our wrongs go unpunished. (I am very grateful for not receiving tickets for all the stop signs I have rolled through when no one was looking.)

Our injustices in life are not about God running some sort of cause-and-effect system of justice. Jesus' healing of the blind man reveals how blind we are to who God really is. The story of the healing is more about opening the eyes of the disciples than healing the eyes of a blind man. It was *their* blindness to the future of God's justice that Jesus was trying to cure. Jesus was shining the light of his life on the ongoing restorative work of God that will reach its fullness in the future.

If anyone can understand the value of injustice, Jesus can. He gets it. He understands how injustice can make it possible for justice to shine brightly. In the light of a lifetime, injustice is what it is, unjust. But when seen as a sign of what is to come, injustice becomes a beacon of hope, shining with potential and meaning. Injustice isn't punishment being delivered; it is a stage for God's justice to star in the leading role. "He was born blind so that God's works might be revealed in him" (3b).

So it is. Jesus sees hope through the injustices in our lives. Hope that the Creator can be seen more clearly. Hope that we would look past the easy understanding of our self-defined fairness and look into the future of God's justice. This story dares us to look past the miracle of restored sight and see the God who likes to get his hands dirty, the God who doesn't mind being connected to the chaos of injustice in this world, the God who isn't threatened by temporarily being misunderstood because of his confidence that soon we, too, will see.

Jesus doesn't settle for the easy way—this life is so much deeper than that. God doesn't look at our brokenness and sin as a problem but as an opportunity to demonstrate himself to the world. What then, should we continue to sin so that God may be magnified even more—of course not! Should we take confidence in a God who can take all of our brokenness and turn it into beauty? Yes!

The disciples were challenged to shift their minds to an understanding that life won't be fair—and that's good. We are challenged to embrace the injustices of our lives as darkness that has yet to be exposed to light. To have bold confidence that where there is injustice, there is a God working through his created elements to restore order.

The blind man speaks.

I was blind, but now I see. Injustice is reversed. A life is healed, restored. The sinner is forgiven. The blind can see. The dead now live. That's God's future. Can we see it? —SA

After reading the passage from John 9 and the devotional reflection "Blind, but Now I See!" you may also want to read the following related passages:

1 Samuel 16:1-13; Psalm 23; Ephesians 5:8-14

The **discussion prompts** that follow will help prepare you to participate in your Sunday school class or small-group study. Use your **reflective journaling**

section to record any other insights that come to you as you read the Gospel lesson and the devotional reflection.

DISCUSSION PROMPT #1: JOHN 9

Do people still associate disease and disability with punishment for sin? Explain.

DISCUSSION PROMPT #2: JOHN 9

How do you feel about Jesus' statement, "He was born blind so that God's works might be revealed in him" (v. 3b)?

DISCUSSION PROMPT #3: JOHN 9

Where would you place your reaction to Jesus' statement on a scale ranging from "absurd" to "awesome"?

DISCUSSION PROMPT #4: DEVOTIONAL REFLECTION

What does the devotional writer mean when he says that this healing had more to do with opening the eyes of the disciples than the eyes of the blind man?

DISCUSSION PROMPT #5: JOHN 9

What sense of urgency do Jesus' comments about working "while it is day" (v. 4) instill in you? How can that sense change the way you currently do things?

REFLECTIVE JOURNALING

_____

_____

_____

_____

_____

_____

_____

_____

_____

MONDAY

WEEK 4
LENTEN SEASON

PSALM 89 ▪ JEREMIAH 14:1-9; 16:10-18, 21 ▪ ROMANS 7:1-12 ▪ JOHN 6:1-15

MORNING MEDITATIONS

PRAYER—Eternal and loving Father, whose blessed Son Jesus Christ came down from heaven to be the true bread which gives life to the world, feed me on this bread that he may live in me and I in him. Amen.

PSALM 89:1-2—I will sing of your steadfast love, O LORD, forever; with my mouth I will proclaim your faithfulness to all generations. I declare that your steadfast love is established forever; your faithfulness is as firm as the heavens.

JEREMIAH 16:15b, 21   *They Shall Know My Name*
I will bring them back to their own land that I gave to their ancestors . . . this time I am going to teach them my power and my might, and they shall know my name is the LORD.

ROMANS 7:4   *Belonging to Christ*
You have died to the law through the body of Christ, so that you may belong to another, to him who has been raised from the dead in order that we may bear fruit for God.

JOHN 6:1-15   *Today's Gospel Reading*

You have turned to Christ, the true high priest, who by means of his blood obtained God's mercy for you and reconciled you with the Father . . . listen to him telling you, "This is my blood which will be poured out for the forgiveness of sins."

A READING FROM THE HOMILIES OF ORIGEN ON THE BOOK OF LEVITICUS

EVENING REFLECTIONS

PSALM 89:5-6, 8—Let the heavens praise your wonders, O LORD, your faithfulness in the assembly of the holy ones. For who in the skies can be compared to the LORD? Who among the heavenly beings is like the LORD . . . who is as mighty as you, O LORD? Your faithfulness surrounds you.

PRAYER—Lord, make me an instrument of Thy peace. Where there is hatred, let me sow love; where there is injury, pardon; where there is doubt, faith; where there is despair, hope. Amen.   ATTRIBUTED TO FRANCIS OF ASSISI

66   ASHES ᴛᴏ FIRE

PSALM 97 • JEREMIAH 17:19-27 • ROMANS 7:13-25 • JOHN 6:16-27

MORNING MEDITATIONS

PRAYER—Eternal and loving Father, whose blessed Son Jesus Christ came down from heaven to be the true bread which gives life to the world, feed me on this bread that he may live in me and I in him. Amen.

PSALM 97:1, 11-12—The LORD is king! Let the earth rejoice . . . Light dawns for the righteous, and joy for the upright in heart. Rejoice in the LORD, O you righteous, and give thanks to his holy name!

JEREMIAH 17:9-10   *The Lord Searches the Heart*
The heart is devious above all else; it is perverse—who can understand it? I the LORD test the mind and search the heart, to give to all according to their ways, according to the fruit of their doings.

ROMANS 7:24-25   *Jesus Saves*
Wretched man that I am! Who will rescue me from this body of death? Thanks be to God through Jesus Christ our Lord!.

JOHN 6:16-27   *Today's Gospel Reading*

So our Lord . . . spoke with blessed mercy, in fulfillment of what had been promised by the prophet Jeremiah: "Behold the days are coming, says the Lord, when I will make a new covenant with Israel and with Judah. . . I will put my law within them and I will write it upon their hearts."   A READING FROM A SERMON BY LEO THE GREAT ON THE BEATITUDES

EVENING REFLECTIONS

PSALM 94:12, 13a, 18-19—Happy are those whom you discipline, O LORD, and whom you teach out of your law, giving them respite from days of trouble . . . When I thought, "My foot is slipping," your steadfast love, O LORD, held me up . . . your consolations cheer my soul.

PRAYER—Lord, make me an instrument of Thy peace. Where there is hatred, let me sow love . . . Where there is darkness, light; where there is sadness, joy. Amen.

ATTRIBUTED TO FRANCIS OF ASSISI

PSALM 101 ▪ JEREMIAH 18:1-11 ▪ ROMANS 8:1-11 ▪ JOHN 6:27-40

MORNING MEDITATIONS

PRAYER—Eternal and loving Father, whose blessed Son Jesus Christ came down from heaven to be the true bread which gives life to the world, feed me on this bread that he may live in me and I in him. Amen.

PSALM 101:1-3—I will sing of loyalty and of justice; to you, O LORD, I will sing. I will study the way that is blameless . . . I will walk with integrity of heart within my house; I will not set before my eyes anything that is base.

JEREMIAH 18:5-6 *Clay in the Potter's Hand*
Then the word of the LORD came to me: Can I not do with you, O house of Israel, just as this potter has done? says the LORD. Just like the clay in the potter's hand, so are you in my hand, O house of Israel.

ROMANS 8:6, 7a, 9a *Set the Mind on the Spirit*
To set the mind on the flesh is death, but to set the mind on the Spirit is life and peace. For this reason the mind that is set on the flesh is hostile to God . . . But you are not in the flesh; you are in the Spirit, since the Spirit of God dwells in you.

JOHN 6:27-40 *Today's Gospel Reading*

The apostles . . . left all of their possessions at once at the call of their heavenly Master. By a sudden conversion they were changed from fishermen to fishers of men, and they called many others to follow their example by imitating their faith.

A READING FROM A SERMON BY LEO THE GREAT ON THE BEATITUDES

EVENING REFLECTIONS

PSALM 119:124-125, 135—Deal with your servant according to your steadfast love, and teach me your statutes. I am your servant; give me understanding so that I may know your decrees . . . Make your face shine upon your servant, and teach me your commandments.

PRAYER—Lord, make me an instrument of Thy peace; where there is hatred, let me sow love . . . O Divine Master, grant that I may not so much seek to be consoled as to console, to be understood, as to understand, to be loved, as to love. Amen.

ATTRIBUTED TO FRANCIS OF ASSISI

PSALM 69 ▪ JEREMIAH 20:7-13; 22:13-23 ▪ ROMANS 8:12-27 ▪ JOHN 6:41-51

MORNING MEDITATIONS

PRAYER—Eternal and Loving Father, whose blessed Son Jesus Christ came down from heaven to be the true bread which gives life to the world, feed me on this bread that he may live in me and I in him. Amen.

PSALM 69:30, 31a, 32, 35a—I will praise the name of God with a song; I will magnify him with thanksgiving. This will please the LORD . . . Let the oppressed see it and be glad; you who seek God, let your hearts revive . . . for God will save Zion.

JEREMIAH 20:12-13   *God Tests the Righteous*
O LORD of hosts, you test the righteous; you see the heart and the mind; let me see your retribution upon them, for to you I have committed my cause. Sing to the LORD; praise the LORD! For he has delivered the life of the needy from the hands of evildoers.

ROMANS 8:26-27   *God Searches the Heart*
Likewise the Spirit helps us in our weakness; for we do not know how to pray as we ought, but that very Spirit intercedes with sighs too deep for words. And God, who searches the heart, knows what is the mind of the Spirit, because the Spirit intercedes for the saints according to the will of God.

JOHN 6:41-51   *Today's Gospel Reading*

The only reason why the saints have to die in the flesh is that Christ through the Holy Spirit has begun to live his life in them. The effect of Christ and his life on the saints is that they die after the flesh . . . Every day Christ is their death and Christ is their life.

A READING FROM *THE COST OF DISCIPLESHIP* BY DIETRICH BONHOEFFER

EVENING REFLECTIONS

PSALM 71:1, 3, 17-18a—In you, O LORD, I take refuge; let me never be put to shame . . . Be to me a rock of refuge, a strong fortress to save me . . . O God, from my youth you have taught me, and I still proclaim your wondrous deeds. So even to old age and gray hairs, O God, do not forsake me.

PRAYER—Lord, make me an instrument of Thy peace; where there is hatred, let me sow love . . . For it is in giving, that we receive, it is in pardoning, that we are pardoned, it is in dying, that we are born to eternal life. Amen.   ATTRIBUTED TO FRANCIS OF ASSISI

PSALM 102 ▪ JEREMIAH 23:1-8 ▪ ROMANS 8:28-39 ▪ JOHN 6:52-59

MORNING MEDITATIONS

PRAYER—Our Father in heaven, whose blessed Son Jesus Christ came down from heaven to be the true bread which gives life to the world, feed me on this bread that he may live in me and I in him. Amen.

PSALM 102:1-2—Hear my prayer, O Lᴏʀᴅ; let my cry come to you. Do not hide your face from me in the day of my distress. Incline your ear to me; answer me speedily in the day when I call.

JEREMIAH 23:5-6   *The Righteous Branch*
The days are surely coming, says the Lᴏʀᴅ, when I will raise up for David a righteous Branch, and he shall reign as king and deal wisely, and shall execute justice and righteousness in the land . . . And this is the name by which he will be called: "The Lᴏʀᴅ is our righteousness."

ROMANS 8:31-32   *God's Love in Christ*
What then are we to say about these things? If God is for us, who is against us? He who did not withhold his own Son, but gave him up for all of us, will he not with him also give us everything else?

JOHN 6:52-59   *Today's Gospel Reading*

It was not enough for God to give us his Son merely to point out the way. He made the Son himself the way, so that you might journey with him as your guide, as he walks in his own way.   A READING FROM AUGUSTINE'S DISCOURSES ON THE PSALMS

EVENING REFLECTIONS

PSALM 102:25-27—Long ago you laid the foundation of the earth, and the heavens are the work of your hands. They will perish, but you endure; they will all wear out like a garment . . . but you are the same and your years have no end.

PRAYER—Father, accept my imperfect repentance, have compassion on my infirmities, forgive my faults, purify my uncleanness, strengthen my weakness, fix my unstableness, and let your good Spirit watch over me forever, and your love ever rule in my heart, through the merits and sufferings and love of your Son, in whom you are always well pleased. Amen. *JW*

SATURDAY

PSALM 108:1-6 ▪ JEREMIAH 23:9-15 ▪ ROMANS 9:1-18 ▪ JOHN 6:60-71

MORNING MEDITATIONS

PRAYER—Our Father in heaven, whose blessed Son Jesus Christ came down from heaven to be the true bread which gives life to the world, feed me on this bread that he may live in me and I in him. Amen.

PSALM 108:1-3a, 5—My heart is steadfast, O God, my heart is steadfast . . . Awake, O harp and lyre! I will awake the dawn. I will give thanks to you, O Lord, among the peoples . . . Be exalted, O God, above the heavens, and let your glory be over all the earth.

JEREMIAH 23:24, 29 *God Fills the Heaven and Earth*
Who can hide in secret places so that I cannot see them? says the Lord. Do I not fill the heaven and earth? says the Lord . . . Is not my word like fire, says the Lord, and like a hammer that breaks a rock in pieces?

ROMANS 9:14-15 *Set the Mind on the Spirit*
What are we to say? Is there injustice on God's part? By no means! For he says to Moses, "I will have mercy on whom I have mercy, and I will have compassion on whom I have compassion."

JOHN 6:60-71 *Today's Gospel Reading*

Mercy demands that you be merciful, righteousness that you be righteous, so that the Creator may be shown forth in the creature and that, in the mirror of man's heart as in the lines of a portrait, the image of God may be reflected.

A READING FROM A SERMON BY LEO THE GREAT ON THE BEATITUDES

EVENING REFLECTIONS

PSALM 33:13-15, 18, 22—The Lord looks down from heaven; he sees all humankind. From where he sits enthroned he watches all the inhabitants of the earth—he who fashions the hearts of all, and observes their deeds. . . . Truly the eye of the Lord is on those who fear him . . . Let your steadfast love, O Lord, be upon us.

PRAYER—Now to God the Father who first loved us, and made us accepted in the Beloved: to God the Son who loved us and washed us from our sins in his own blood; to God the Holy Spirit who fills our hearts with the love of God, be all love and all glory for time and for eternity. Amen. **JW**

WEEK FIVE
Lenten Season

Sunday: With Jesus in a Cemetery

*Read the Gospel passage from John 11:1-45, the devotional reflection
titled "Jesus—Resurrection Life," and respond to the discussion
prompts in the Reflective Journaling section.*

THE MUSIC OF ASHES TO FIRE

Week 5: "Dry Bones" (Track 6)

Monday through Saturday of Week 5

IN THE MORNING:

*A personal daily devotional guide includes prayer,
a reading from the Old Testament, the Psalms, the Epistles,
and the Gospel for each day of the week.*

*This week's readings are from Jeremiah,
Romans, and the Gospel of John.*

*Inspirational quotes from men and women of faith
keep us in contact with our shared Christian heritage.*

IN THE EVENING:

*An evening psalm and prayer become preludes
to nighttime rest and renewal.*

LENTEN SEASON–WEEK FIVE
With Jesus in a Cemetery

A devotional reflection based on John 11:1-45

Read the Gospel passage first, then the devotional reflection that follows. The discussion prompts at the end will help prepare you for Sunday school and small-group sessions.

Jesus—Resurrection Life

Death precedes life.

It seems absurd just to write that sentence. We know it's not true. Life itself teaches us that death is inescapable. Just yesterday I stood beside the bed of a dying man. And this morning I learned he had died in the night. It was inevitable. I knew, he knew, and the family knew he would die. So let's just admit it: life precedes death, and death is inevitable.

Martha knew it. She understood Lazarus was dead. And she understood the permanence of death. The reality of death's pending finality led to the urgent message requesting Jesus to come visit Lazarus while he was still sick. Martha believed that Jesus could heal sickness, but death, death was final, right?

Certainly, after Lazarus had died, she didn't dare to presuppose that Jesus could do anything about it. You can hear in her response that hope had died with the last breath of Lazarus. She hopelessly declared to the late-arriving Jesus, "If only you had been here."

Then Jesus, always looking for an opportunity to teach, responded to her hopelessness by asking Martha to examine her own beliefs. "Your brother will rise again," Jesus replied, referring to the common Jewish belief (except for the Sadducees) that all of God's people would rise to live in the new heavens and new earth described by Isaiah (chaps. 65 and 66).

Martha reluctantly affirmed her belief in this future resurrection: "I know he will rise again in the resurrection at the last day." But clearly this wasn't the comfort or hope Martha was looking for.

We can understand Martha's frustration. We too often try to walk forward through life while staring back over our shoulder at certain mistakes or events we wish had turned out differently. We grow frustrated at the constant disappointment and accompanying letdown of our faith in a God who loves. We, like Martha, want to believe that if God loves us so much, surely he will drop what he is doing and run to where we are to fix our situation.

Jesus then challenged Martha to accept another reality: "*I am* the resurrection and the life," he said.

Wait a second. *You*, Jesus, are the Resurrection? The Resurrection is not just an event, or a belief, but a *person*?

This part of the story is so foreign to our reality that we, like Martha, might easily miss the meaning behind it. We unknowingly focus in on our present reality without recognizing God's future standing right in front of us in the form of the person, Jesus. We tend to focus on the amazing and almost unbelievable part of the story of a dead man being raised from his tomb, and if we aren't attentive, we might look past the Resurrection to see resurrection.

But the Teacher, not wanting us to miss the opportunity to understand, asks us directly, "Do you believe?" Do we believe that Jesus is the Resurrection? Do we believe that Jesus brings life out of death? Do we believe that death precedes life?

It is what Jesus asked of Martha, "Do you believe?" Do you believe that Jesus, the Resurrection, is present right now, right here in front of you? Can you dare to believe that the Resurrection will bring life out of death? Do you believe the future is now present?

What if we actually believed in the Resurrection? What if we really understood that Jesus is the Resurrection? What if Jesus was not only a historical fact—someone who was born in a manger, lived 2,010 years ago, and died on a cross? What if Jesus is the future resurrection standing right in front of us today, begging us to answer this simple question, "Do you believe death precedes life?"

It changes everything when the Resurrection moves from a future event to the present reality of the indwelling presence of Jesus. Suddenly we are made aware of resurrection all around us and in us, right here, right now. We become witnesses of dead hope rising from its resting place of convinced impossibility and changing into the certainty of present reality. We see resurrection in the lives of new believers, in the restoration of the offended, in the renewal of addicts, in the faces of the hopeless. We testify that faith is the lens through which we can see the future.

What if Jesus' self-imposed nickname stuck? Jesus, also known as the Resurrection. Would our understanding of the mission of God become clearer if we switched the saying from, "What would Jesus do?" to "What would Resurrection do?" Or how about instead of saying, "I want to be like Jesus," we said, "I want to be like the Resurrection."

What if we lived with this resurrection attitude? What would happen if we lived out the Resurrection? It would change everything. It would eliminate the sting of death, sorrow, and suffering. We would embrace life differently—seeing hopelessness as hope in the making, mourning as joy, sickness as healing, disappointment as fulfillment, and death as life. Resurrection living leads us directly into Christlikeness.

This kind of faith is a vital sign of hope and confidence in a God who loves. We hear Jesus ask us, as he did Martha, "Do you believe?" If we live in this resurrection power, we discover that our future hope already exists in the here and now and that our present relationship with God through Christ is future reality. Our declared impossibilities must be questioned. Our doubts must die and rise into faith. "If only Jesus would have . . . ," must awaken and rise into, "Jesus already has . . ."

Resurrection life is invincible. Resurrection power can't die. Resurrection hope lives in me. Resurrection faith changes everything.

Do you believe? —SA

After reading the passage from John 11 and the devotional reflection "Jesus—Resurrection Life" you may also want to read the following related passages:
Joel 2:1-2, 12-17; Psalm 51:1-17; 2 Corinthians 5:20b—6:10

The **discussion prompts** that follow will help prepare you to participate in your Sunday school class or small-group study. Use your **reflective journaling** section to record any other insights that come to you as you read the Gospel lesson and the devotional reflection.

DISCUSSION PROMPT #1: JOHN 11

What do you notice about Jesus' responses to the different questions asked of him by Mary, Martha, and the crowd of people? Are they on the same page?

DISCUSSION PROMPT #2: JOHN 11

How do you feel about Jesus using Lazarus' death to reveal God's glory and to teach the disciples and the crowd to believe? Do you think that his was a proper response to the tremendous grief of these people? Explain.

DISCUSSION PROMPT #3: JOHN 11

Throughout this passage, first Martha, then Mary, and finally the crowd complained that Jesus could have saved Lazarus from death if he had acted as they thought he should. Is that a common attitude among Christians today?

DISCUSSION PROMPT #4: DEVOTIONAL REFLECTION

The devotional writer suggests a shift from thinking of resurrection as "future event" to thinking about resurrection as a Living Person, a present reality—namely, Jesus. How does that encourage and strengthen your faith?

REFLECTIVE JOURNALING

_____

_____

_____

_____

_____

_____

_____

_____

_____

_____

_____

_____

PSALM 31 ▪ **JEREMIAH 24:1-10** ▪ **ROMANS 9:19-33** ▪ **JOHN 9:1-17**

MORNING MEDITATIONS

PRAYER—Almighty God, you alone can bring into order all the unruly affections of my life. I pray that you will give me grace to love what you command and desire what you promise so that my heart may be focused where true joy is found. In the name and for the sake of Jesus Christ, I pray. Amen. **JW**

PSALM 31:14-16—I trust in you, O Lord; I say, "You are my God." My times are in your hand; deliver me from [the enemy]. Let your face shine upon your servant; save me in your steadfast love.

JEREMIAH 24:4a, 7 *A New Heart*
Then the word of the Lord came to me . . . I will give them a heart to know that I am the Lord; and they shall be my people and I will be their God, for they shall return to me with their whole heart.

ROMANS 9:25-26 *Children of the Living God*
As indeed he says in Hosea, "Those who were not my people I will call 'my people,' and her who was not beloved I will call 'beloved.' And in the very place where it was said to them, 'You are not my people,' there they shall be called children of the living God."

JOHN 9:1-17 *Today's Gospel Reading*

Mercy demands that you be merciful, righteousness that you be righteous, so that the Creator may be shown forth in the creature and that, in the mirror of man's heart as in the lines of a portrait, the image of God may be reflected.

A READING FROM A SERMON BY LEO THE GREAT ON THE BEATITUDES

EVENING REFLECTIONS

PSALM 119:124-125, 135—Deal with your servant according to your steadfast love, and teach me your statutes. I am your servant; give me understanding, so that I may know your decrees . . . Make your face shine upon your servant, and teach me your statutes.

PRAYER—O God, fill my soul with so entire a love for you, that I may love nothing but you. Give me grace to study your knowledge daily, that the more I know you, the more I may love you, through Jesus Christ my Lord. Amen. **JW**

TUESDAY

PSALM 121 ▪ JEREMIAH 30:1-11 ▪ ROMANS 10:1-13 ▪ JOHN 9:18-41

MORNING MEDITATIONS

PRAYER—Eternal and Merciful Father, I give you humble thanks for all the spiritual and earthly blessings which in your mercy you have poured into my life. Lord, let me live only to love you and glorify your name. Amen. *JW*

PSALM 121:1-2, 5—I lift up my eyes to the hills—from where will my help come? My help comes from the LORD, who made heaven and earth . . . The LORD is your keeper; the LORD is your shade at your right hand.

JEREMIAH 30:10-11a   *I Will Save You*
But as for you, have no fear, my servant Jacob, says the LORD, and do not be dismayed, O Israel; for I am going to save you from far away . . . For I am with you, says the LORD, to save you.

ROMANS 10:9-10   *Set the Mind on the Spirit*
If you confess with your lips that Jesus is Lord and believe in your heart that God raised him from the dead, you will be saved. For one believes with the heart and so is justified, and one confesses with the mouth and so is saved.

JOHN 9:18-41   *Today's Gospel Reading*

All the more wonderful is the mercy of God towards us, because Christ died not for the just or the holy, but for the unrighteous . . . He threatened our death with the power of his death . . . but by rising he destroyed its power.

A READING FROM SERMON 8 BY LEO THE GREAT ON THE CROSS OF CHRIST

EVENING REFLECTIONS

PSALM 121:3a, 4, 7a, 8—[The LORD] will not let your foot be moved . . . He who keeps Israel will neither slumber nor sleep. . . . The LORD will keep you from all evil . . . The LORD will keep your going out and your coming in from this time on and forevermore.

PRAYER—O Lamb of God, give me grace throughout my whole life, in every thought, and word and work, to imitate your meekness and humility. May I go through all the scenes of life not seeking my own glory, but looking wholly unto you, and acting wholly for you, through Christ my Lord. Amen. *JW*

WEDNESDAY

WEEK 5
LENTEN SEASON

PSALM 119:145-176 ▪ JEREMIAH 31:1-14 ▪ ROMANS 10:14-21 ▪ JOHN 10:1-18

MORNING MEDITATIONS

PRAYER—O God, fill me with confidence and trust that in knowing your will, I may follow it, and that in following your will, I will find joy, through Jesus Christ, my Lord. Amen.

PSALM 119:145-148—With my whole heart I cry; answer me, O Lord . . . I cry to you: save me, that I may observe your decrees. I rise before dawn and cry for help; I put my hope in your words. My eyes are awake . . . that I may meditate on your promise.

JEREMIAH 31:7, 10c *Shepherd of the Flock*
For thus says the Lord: Sing aloud with gladness for Jacob, and raise shouts for the chief of nations; proclaim, give praise, and say, "Save, O Lord, your people, the remnant of Israel" . . . He who scattered Israel will gather him and will keep him as a shepherd a flock.

ROMANS 10:16-17 *Faith Comes by Hearing*
Not all have obeyed the good news; for Isaiah says, "Lord, who has believed our message?" So faith comes from what is heard, and what is heard comes through the word of Christ.

JOHN 10:1-18 *Today's Gospel Reading*

Faith in the sense of a particular divine grace conferred by the Spirit is not primarily concerned with doctrine but with giving man powers which are quite beyond his capability . . . In a flash faith can produce the most wonderful effects in the soul . . . making good the rewards God promised.   A READING FROM THE INSTRUCTIONS OF CYRIL OF JERUSALEM

EVENING REFLECTIONS

PSALM 80:1, 2b, 7—Give ear, O Shepherd of Israel, you who lead Joseph like a flock! . . . Stir up your might, and come to save us! . . . Restore us, O God of hosts; let your face shine, that we may be saved.

PRAYER—Father, grant me forgiveness of what is past, that in the days to come I may with a pure spirit do your will—walking humbly with you, showing love to all, and keeping body and soul in sanctification and honor, in Jesus' name. Amen.

THURSDAY

PSALM 131 ▪ JEREMIAH 31:15-26 ▪ ROMANS 11:1-24 ▪ JOHN 10:19-42

MORNING MEDITATIONS

PRAYER—O Eternal God, my Savior and Lord, I acknowledge that all I am and all I have is yours. I pray that you will surround me with such a sense of your infinite goodness, that I may return to you all possible love and obedience, through Jesus Christ, Amen. **JW**

PSALM 131—O Lord, my heart is not lifted up, my eyes are not raised too high . . . but I have calmed and quieted my soul like a weaned child with its mother . . . O Israel, hope in the Lord from this time on and forevermore.

JEREMIAH 31:18 *Bring Me Back*
Indeed I heard Ephraim pleading: "You disciplined me, and I took the discipline; I was like a calf untrained. Bring me back, let me come back, for you are the Lord my God.

ROMANS 11:20c-22a *The Kindness of God*
So do not become proud, but stand in awe. For if God did not spare the natural branches, perhaps he will not spare you. Note then the kindness and the severity of God: severity toward those who have fallen, but God's kindness toward you.

JOHN 10:19-42 *Today's Gospel Reading*

Therefore, whoever would teach as the scriptures do, and especially whoever would teach as Christ does, must be careful to show people both sides of the picture; he must tell of judgment as well as mercy; he must always temper fear with love.

A READING FROM A SERMON BY JOHN KEBLE

EVENING REFLECTIONS

PSALM 140:12-13—I know that the Lord maintains the cause of the needy, and executes justice for the poor. Surely the righteous shall give thanks to your name; the upright shall live in your presence.

PRAYER—Protect me, Lord, as I stay awake; watch over me as I sleep, that awake, I may keep watch with Christ, and asleep, rest in his peace. Amen.

PSALM 22 ▪ JEREMIAH 31:27-33 ▪ ROMANS 11:25-36 ▪ JOHN 11:1-27

MORNING MEDITATIONS

PRAYER—Our Father in heaven, whose blessed Son Jesus Christ came down from heaven to be the true bread which gives life to the world, feed me on this bread that he may live in me and I in him. Amen.

PSALM 22:3-5—You are holy, enthroned on the praises of Israel. In you our ancestors trusted; they trusted, and you delivered them. To you they cried, and were saved; in you they trusted, and were not put to shame.

JEREMIAH 31:33 *God Fills the Heaven and Earth*
This is the covenant I will make with the house of Israel . . . , says the LORD: I will put my law within them, and I will write it on their hearts; and I will be their God, and they shall be my people.

ROMANS 11:33, 36 *Set the Mind on the Spirit*
O the depth of the riches and wisdom and knowledge of God! How unsearchable are his judgments and how inscrutable his ways . . . For from him and through him and to him are all things. To him be the glory forever. Amen.

JOHN 11:1-27 *Today's Gospel Reading*

He it is . . . who at the same time is priest through which we are reconciled, the sacrifice by which we are reconciled, the temple in which we are reconciled, the God to whom we are reconciled. He alone is priest, sacrifice, and temple because he is all these as God according to the form of a servant. AN EXCERPT FROM A TREATISE BY FULGENTIUS OF RUSPE

EVENING REFLECTIONS

PSALM 141:1-2—I call upon you, O LORD; come quickly to me; give ear to my voice when I call to you. Let my prayer be counted as incense before you, and the lifting up of my hands as an evening sacrifice.

PRAYER—Almighty God, your love for us is more than we could ever imagine. Fill our lives with your love, our minds with your thoughts, our mouths with your truth, so that every part of our living is touched by your grace. Amen.

PSALM 145 ▪ JEREMIAH 31:34-40 ▪ ROMANS 12:1-8 ▪ JOHN 11:28-44

MORNING MEDITATIONS

PRAYER—Our Father in heaven, whose blessed Son Jesus Christ came down from heaven to be the true bread which gives life to the world, feed me on this bread that he may live in me and I in him. Amen.

PSALM 145:8-9—The Lord is gracious and merciful, slow to anger and abounding in steadfast love. The Lord is good to all, and his compassion is over all that he has made.

JEREMIAH 31:34 *I Will Forgive Their Sin*
No longer shall they teach one another, or say to each other, "Know the Lord," for they shall all know me, from the least of them to the greatest, says the Lord; for I will forgive their iniquity, and remember their sin no more.

ROMANS 12:1 *Set the Mind on the Spirit*
I appeal to you therefore, brothers and sisters, by the mercies of God, to present your bodies as a living sacrifice, holy and acceptable to God, which is your spiritual worship.

JOHN 11:28-44 *Today's Gospel Reading*

To say something greater still, let us sacrifice ourselves to God; further let us go on every day offering ourselves and all our activities. Let us accept everything literally, let us imitate the passion by our sufferings, let us reverence the blood by our blood, let us be eager to climb the cross.   A READING FROM GREGORY OF NAZIANZUS

EVENING REFLECTIONS

PSALM 119:124-125, 135—Deal with your servant according to your steadfast love, and teach me your statutes. I am your servant; give me understanding so that I may know your decrees . . . Make your face shine upon your servant, and teach me your statutes.

PRAYER—Now to God the Father who first loved us, and made us accepted in the Beloved: to God the Son who loved us and washed us from our sins in his own blood; to God the Holy Spirit who fills our hearts with the love of God, be all love and all glory for time and for eternity. Amen. *JW*

WEEK SIX
LENTEN SEASON

Sunday: With Jesus on the Way to Calvary

Read the Gospel passage from Matthew 21:1-11, the devotional reflection titled "What Are You Cheering About?" and respond to the discussion prompts in the Reflective Journaling section.

THE MUSIC OF ASHES TO FIRE

Week 6: "Here Comes the King" (Track 7)

Monday through Saturday of Week 6

IN THE MORNING:

A personal daily devotional guide includes prayer, a reading from the Old Testament, the Psalms, the Epistles, and the Gospel for each day of the week.

This week's readings are from Genesis, Job, Jeremiah, Philippians, I Corinthians, Hebrews, I Peter, and the Gospel of John.

Inspirational quotes from men and women of faith keep us in contact with our shared Christian heritage.

IN THE EVENING:

An evening psalm and prayer become preludes to nighttime rest and renewal.

*L*ENTEN *S*EASON–*WEEK* SIX
With Jesus on the Way to Calvary

A devotional reflection based on Matthew 21:1-11

*R*ead the Gospel passage first, then the devotional reflection that follows. The discussion prompts at the end will help prepare you for Sunday school and small-group sessions.

What Are You Cheering About?

With the anticipation of Easter Day building, we (in the Northern Hemisphere) also enjoy the arrival of spring. One of my spring enjoyments is the beginning of baseball. While living near Chicago, a favorite activity of mine was to visit Wrigley Field, home of the Chicago Cubs. One particular visit stands out in my memory.

Arriving a little late that day, I had just crested the top of the stairs at the entrance to the field box seats when suddenly the crowd erupted in cheers and applause. Apparently something had happened on the field just prior to the game beginning that had people out of their seats and roaring. I quickly located my numbered place to find the man assigned to the adjacent seat going wild with cheers, whistles, and applause. I poked him on the shoulder and asked, "What happened?" Without the slightest embarrassment he said, "I don't know; I just got here."

Sometimes, we just get caught up in the cheer, don't we? There is such a thing as crowd mentality, and probably none of us is completely beyond the possibility of being drawn into it. Our Bible story seems to have something to do with the capricious nature of crowds.

This is a wonderful story. The images are so vibrant we can almost place ourselves among the throng as Jesus enters the city. We can see the waving palm branches and hear the happy cries of the people as they welcome the coming

King. We are moved as we see in our mind's eye people taking off their cloaks and lining the road with them for the Messiah. It is a scene that is being replayed these days in countless passion plays and Easter pageants all over the world. We know this story very well.

There is a part of this story, however, that has always muted the exuberance of it for me. It is that I have read ahead and know that in just a short time this very crowd will be screaming, "Crucify him!" As John tells this story, he says of the disciples who were as caught up in the moment as anyone, "The disciples didn't understand all of this." We know this is true. In fact, it was only after Jesus was glorified and the Holy Spirit came upon them that they finally put two and two together and suddenly the lights went on. So the question strikes me, "If these disciples didn't understand what was happening, then what in the world was the crowd cheering about?"

If these who had been with Jesus constantly and been under his teaching were not appreciating the real meaning of this event, then what are we to believe about why this great throng was hailing Jesus as the Messiah? A wider reading of the Gospel begins to reveal to us what they were cheering about.

Jesus was generally acclaimed by the crowds as the hero miracle worker. He is one who could heal, cast out demons, and make bread for crowds. At times they were ready to make him king on the spot. So when Jesus comes into Jerusalem, his public approval rating is off the charts. All over Jerusalem people were looking for him and asking about him. He was a hero. Word got out that he was coming into the city, so the crowds went out from Jerusalem toward Bethphage with palm branches heralding the arrival—of whom? The hero. The miracle worker. The magic Messiah who would grant them all their wishes. Jesus was doing, they thought, exactly what they had always wanted him to do. He is riding into the city as a king to proclaim his rule and reign. Perhaps they didn't notice that Jesus wasn't riding a white stallion, the sign of a conquering warrior. He was on a donkey, a symbol of peace. He wasn't coming to overthrow the government or the religious system per se. He knew, and apparently was the only one who really knew, that he was headed for a cross.

We've seen this crowd before, haven't we? This fickle crowd one minute cheering and the next minute jeering. Here, it "seems as if the whole world has gone after him," but in a very short while he will die a criminal's death mostly alone. They really didn't know what they were cheering for, did they? Their acclamation was correct. They spoke the right words. They just didn't understand what they were saying.

I imagine looking into the faces of this crowd—this mindless, happy-go-lucky crowd that is so ready for a party, ready to sing, "Happy days are here again." They think they are joining the parade of a victorious soldier and do not realize they are really marching in a funeral procession. Yet as I look at them, wondering how they could be so shallow, suddenly I see my own face. How often do I clamor after the superstar Jesus? How often do I have false, unholy expectations of what Jesus will do for me? How often do I see him as my divine errand boy who will make my way easy and comfortable?

When this is our picture of Jesus, it's pretty easy to be part of the cheering crowd. Who couldn't get excited about following a Jesus like that? But suddenly the shadow of a cross falls across my path and I stop dead in my tracks. Wait a minute. This isn't what I bargained for. How can I cheer for a Jesus who gets himself killed? How can I cheer for a Jesus who is broken and bruised because of my sin?

In just a short time we will gather to celebrate Easter, proclaiming the glory of our risen Lord. We will sing praises to the Savior who won the victory and now sits at the right hand of God in glory. It's the picture of Jesus we love best—the powerful, beautiful, radiant Jesus. But I would ask us, when we celebrate the victory of Jesus, will we really know what we are cheering about? Will we just be joining the crowd and getting caught up in the emotion of it all? Or will we be able to celebrate with tears of joy because we have been to Golgotha? Will our celebration rise from our having seen the beaten, lonely, pitiful Jesus and realizing that he died there for the love of you and me?

As we approach Easter, it is good to anticipate the celebration. But let us cheer from understanding and from faith. Let us celebrate not only the hero, miracle-worker Jesus but also the crucified and resurrected Lord. An important part of being ready for that is to walk through the days of Holy Week with intention. Make the week truly "holy" by setting these days apart. Live into the way of the cross. Walk with Jesus along the *Via Dolorosa*. Somehow, let yourself experience the scandal of the cross. Let yourself feel the heaviness of the Last Supper, the terror of Gethsemane, and the tragedy of Golgotha. If you will, then you can come to Easter knowing from deep inside your heart what you are really cheering about. —JR

After reading the passage from Matthew 21 and the devotional reflection "What Are You Cheering About?" you may also want to read the following related passages:

Isaiah 52:13—53:12; Psalm 118:1-2, 19-29; Philippians 2:5-11

The **discussion prompts** that follow will help prepare you to participate in your Sunday school class or small-group study. Use your **reflective journaling** section to record any other insights that come to you as you read the Gospel lesson and the devotional reflection.

DISCUSSION PROMPT #1: DEVOTIONAL REFLECTION

Was there ever a time when your initial enthusiasm in following Jesus was dampened by the unanticipated "cost" of discipleship? Explain.

DISCUSSION PROMPT #2: MATTHEW 21

The Gospel account quotes an Old Testament passage, Zechariah 9:9. Read from 9:9 through 9:17. How does reading the extended passage better illuminate the significance of Palm Sunday?

DISCUSSION PROMPT #3: MATTHEW 21

Did the crowds understand what the triumphal entry meant? Explain. John 12:18 holds a clue.

DISCUSSION PROMPT #4: MATTHEW 21

Can you think of any current examples of fickle followers?

REFLECTIVE JOURNALING

_____

_____

_____

_____

_____

_____

_____

PSALM 51:1-18 ▪ **JEREMIAH 12:1-6** ▪ **PHILIPPIANS 3:1-11** ▪ **JOHN 12:9-19**

MORNING MEDITATIONS

PRAYER—O God, you are the Giver of all good gifts. I desire to praise your name for all the expressions of your goodness to me, for giving your Son to die for my sins, for the means of grace and for the hope of glory. Amen. *JW*

PSALM 51:8-9—Let me hear joy and gladness; let the bones you have crushed rejoice. Hide your face from my sins, and blot out all my iniquities.

JEREMIAH 12:3 *You Know Me*
But you, O LORD, know me; you see me and test me—my heart is with you.

PHILIPPIANS 3:10-11 *I Want to Know Christ*
I want to know Christ and the power of his resurrection and the sharing of his sufferings by becoming like him in his death, if somehow I may attain the resurrection from the dead.

JOHN 12:9-19 *Today's Gospel Reading*

So far from being ashamed at the death of the Lord our God, we must have the fullest trust in it; it must be our greatest boast, for by assuming from us death, which he found in us, he pledged most faithfully to give us life in himself, which we could not have ourselves.   A READING FROM THE SERMONS OF ST. AUGUSTINE

EVENING REFLECTIONS

PSALM 69:16-18—Answer me, O LORD, for your steadfast love is good; according to your abundant mercy, turn to me. Do not hide your face from your servant, for I am in distress—make haste to answer me. Draw near to me, redeem me, set me free because of my enemies.

PRAYER—O God, fill my soul with so entire a love for you, that I may love nothing but you. Give me grace to study your knowledge daily, that the more I know you, the more I may love you, through Jesus Christ my Lord. Amen. *JW*

PSALM 6 ▪ JEREMIAH 15:10-21 ▪ PHILIPPIANS 3:12-21 ▪ JOHN 12:20-26

MORNING MEDITATIONS

PRAYER—Eternal and merciful Father, I give you humble thanks for all the spiritual and earthly blessings which in your mercy you have poured into my life. Lord, let me live only to love you and glorify your name. Amen. **JW**

PSALM 6:4, 9—Turn, O Lord, save my life; deliver me for the sake of your steadfast love . . . The Lord has heard my supplication; the Lord accepts my prayer.

JEREMIAH 15:15a, 16b-d   *Lord, Remember Me*
O Lord, you know; remember me and visit me . . . your words became to me a joy and the delight of my heart; for I am called by your name, O Lord, God of hosts.

PHILIPPIANS 3:12   *I Press On*
Not that I have already obtained this or have already reached the goal; but I press on to make it my own, because Christ Jesus has made me his own.

JOHN 12:20-26   *Today's Gospel Reading*

This was the purpose of Christ's dwelling in the flesh, the pattern of his life described in the Gospels, his sufferings, the cross, the burial, the resurrection; so that humanity could be saved.   A READING FROM THE BOOK *ON THE HOLY SPIRIT* BY BASIL THE GREAT

EVENING REFLECTIONS

PSALM 94:16-17, 22—Who rises up for me against the wicked? Who stands for me against evildoers? If the Lord had not been my help, my soul would soon have [fainted] . . . But the Lord has become my stronghold, and my God the rock of my refuge.

PRAYER—O Lamb of God, in this evening sacrifice of praise and prayer, I offer you a contrite heart. Give me grace, throughout my whole life, in every thought, and word, and work to imitate your meekness and humility, through Christ, my Lord, I pray. Amen. **JW**

PSALM 55 ▪ JEREMIAH 17:5-18 ▪ PHILIPPIANS 4:1-13 ▪ JOHN 12:27-36

MORNING MEDITATIONS

PRAYER—Lord God, send your Holy Spirit to be the guide of all my ways and the sanctifier of my soul and body. Give me the light of your presence, your peace from heaven, and the salvation of my soul, through Jesus Christ my Lord. Amen.

PSALM 55:4a, 5a, 6, 8—My heart is in anguish within me . . . fear and trembling come upon me . . . and I say, "O that I had wings like a dove! I would fly away and be at rest . . . I would hurry to find a shelter for myself from the raging wind and tempest."

JEREMIAH 17:14, 16a   *I Have Not Run Away from Being a Shepherd*
Heal me, O LORD, and I shall be healed; save me, and I shall be saved; for you are my praise . . . I have not run away from being a shepherd in your service, nor have I desired the fatal day.

PHILIPPIANS 4:11b-12a, 13   *I Can Do All Things Through Christ*
I have learned to be content with whatever I have. I know what it is to have little, and I know what it is to have plenty . . . I can do all things through [Christ] who strengthens me.

JOHN 12:27-36   *Today's Gospel Reading*

He had the power to lay down his life, and to take it again; we, on the other hand, do not live as long as we want to live, and we die even if we do not want to die. He, by dying, at once destroyed death in himself, we are freed from death by his death.

A READING FROM THE SERMONS ON JOHN'S GOSPEL BY ST. AUGUSTINE

EVENING REFLECTIONS

PSALM 74:18a, 20a, 21-22a—Remember this, O LORD, how the enemy scoffs . . . Have regard for your covenant . . . Do not let the downtrodden be put to shame; let the poor and needy praise your name. Rise up, O God, plead your cause.

PRAYER—Father, grant me forgiveness of what is past, that in the days to come I may with a pure spirit do your will—walking humbly with you, showing love to all, and keeping body and soul in sanctification and honor, in Jesus' name. Amen.

PSALM 102 ▪ **JEREMIAH 20:7-13** ▪ **I CORINTHIANS 10:14-17** ▪ **JOHN 17:1-11**

MORNING MEDITATIONS

PRAYER (BCP)—Our Father in heaven, hallowed be your Name,
your kingdom come, your will be done, on earth as in heaven.
Give us today our daily bread.
Forgive us our sins as we forgive those who sin against us.
Save us from the time of trial, and deliver us from evil.
For the kingdom, the power, and the glory are yours, now and for
ever. Amen.

PSALM 102:1-2—Hear my prayer, O Lord; let my cry come to you . . . Incline your ear to me; answer me speedily in the day when I call.

JEREMIAH 20:12a, 13   *Lord, You Test the Righteous*
O Lord of hosts, you test the righteous, you see the heart and the mind . . . Sing to the Lord;
praise the Lord! For he has delivered the life of the needy from the hands of evildoers.

1 CORINTHIANS 10:16b-17   *There Is One Bread*
The bread that we break, is it not a sharing in the body of Christ? Because there is one bread,
we who are many are one body; for we all partake of the one bread.

JOHN 17:1-11   *Today's Gospel Reading*

He is the Passover of our salvation. He was present in many so as to endure many
things. In Abel, he was slain; in Isaac bound; in Jacob a stranger; in Joseph sold; in Moses
exposed; in David persecuted; in the prophets foretold . . . He was seized from the flock
and dragged away to slaughter . . . But he rose from the dead and raised up man from
the depths of the grave.   A READING FROM A SERMON BY MELITO OF SARDIS

EVENING REFLECTIONS

PSALM 142:5—I cry to you, O Lord; I say, "You are my refuge, my portion in the land of the living."

PRAYER—My Lord and my God, you see my heart; and my desires are not hidden from you. I am encouraged and strengthened by your goodness to me today. I want to be yours and yours alone. O my God, my Savior, my Sanctifier, hear me, help me, and show mercy to me for Jesus Christ's sake. Amen. *JW*

PSALM 22 ▪ GENESIS 22:1-14 ▪ 1 PETER 1:10-20 ▪ JOHN 13:36-38

MORNING MEDITATIONS

PRAYER—O God, by the death and resurrection of your Son Jesus Christ, you delivered and saved the world. Grant that by faith in him who suffered on the cross, we may triumph in the power of his victory; through Jesus Christ, our Lord. Amen.

PSALM 22:1, 4, 19—My God, my God, why have you forsaken me? Why are you so far from helping me, from the words of my groaning . . . In you our ancestors trusted; they trusted and you delivered them . . . O Lord, do not be far away! O my help, come quickly to my aid!

GENESIS 22:7-8 *God Will Provide a Lamb*
Isaac said to his father Abraham, . . . "The fire and the wood are here, but where is the lamb for a burnt offering?" Abraham said, "God himself will provide the lamb for a burnt offering, my son." So the two of them walked on together.

1 PETER 1:18-19 *The Precious Blood*
You know that you were ransomed from the futile ways inherited from your ancestors, not with perishable things like silver or gold, but with the precious blood of Christ, like that of a lamb without defect or blemish.

JOHN 13:36-38 *Today's Gospel Reading*

Today there is a great silence over the earth, a great silence and stillness, a great silence because the King sleeps; the earth was in terror and was still, because God slept in the flesh and raised up those who were sleeping from the ages. God has died in the flesh and all hell trembles.
A READING FROM AN ANCIENT SERMON

EVENING REFLECTIONS

PSALM 40:1, 13, 17b—I waited patiently for the Lord; he inclined to me and heard my cry . . . Be pleased, O Lord, to deliver me; O Lord, make haste to help me . . . You are my help and my deliverer; do not delay, O my God.

TONIGHT: Observe silence

PSALM 88 ▪ JOB 19:21-27a ▪ HEBREWS 4:1-16 ▪ ROMANS 8:1-11

MORNING MEDITATIONS

PRAYER—O God, by the death and resurrection of your Son Jesus Christ, you delivered and saved the world. Grant that by faith in him who suffered on the cross, we may triumph in the power of his victory; through Jesus Christ, our Lord. Amen.

PSALM 88:1-2a, 3a, 6, 11a—O LORD, God of my salvation, when, at night, I cry out in your presence, let my prayer come before you . . . For my soul is full of troubles . . . You have put me in the depths of the Pit, in the regions dark and deep . . . Is your steadfast love declared in the grave?

JOB 19:25-27 *I Know My Redeemer Lives*
For I know that my Redeemer lives, and that at the last he will stand upon the earth; and after my skin has been thus destroyed, then in my flesh I shall see God, whom I shall see on my side, and my eyes shall behold.

HEBREWS 4:14-15 *Our Great High Priest*
Since, then, we have a great high priest who has passed through the heavens, Jesus, the Son of God, let us hold fast to our confession. For we do no have a high priest who is unable to sympathize with our weaknesses, but we have one who in every respect has been tested as we are, yet without sin.

ROMANS 8:1-11 *Today's Gospel Reading*

Have you understood the victory? No weapons of ours were stained with blood; our feet did not stand in the front line of battle; we suffered no wounds; witnessed no tumults . . . The cross did all these wonderful things for us: the Cross is a war memorial erected against the demons. The Cross is the Father's will, the glory of the Only-begotten, the Spirit's exultation, the beauty of angels, the guardian of the Church.

A READING FROM A SERMON BY JOHN CHRYSOSTOM

EVENING REFLECTIONS

PSALM 27:13-14—I believe that I shall see the goodness of the LORD in the land of the living. Wait for the LORD; be strong, and let your heart take courage; wait for the LORD!

TONIGHT: Observe silence

EASTER SEASON

Ashes to Fire Week 7

Sunday: With Jesus at the Empty Tomb

*Read the Gospel passages from Matthew 28:1-10 and
John 20:1-18, the devotional reflection titled "Do You Believe?"
and respond to the discussion prompts in the
Reflective Journaling section.*

THE MUSIC OF ASHES TO FIRE

Week 7: "The Empty Tomb" (Track 8)

Monday through Saturday of Easter Season
Week 1

IN THE MORNING:

*A personal daily devotional guide includes prayer,
a reading from the Old Testament, the Psalms, the Epistles,
and the Gospel for each day of the week.*

*This week's readings are from Daniel, I John,
and the Gospel of John.*

*Inspirational quotes from men and women of faith
keep us in contact with our shared Christian heritage.*

IN THE EVENING:

*An evening psalm and prayer become preludes
to nighttime rest and renewal.*

EASTER SEASON—WEEK ONE
With Jesus at the Empty Tomb

A devotional reflection based on Matthew 28:1-10; John 20:1-18

Read the Gospel passage first, then the devotional reflection that follows. The discussion prompts at the end will help prepare you for Sunday school and small-group sessions.

Do You Believe?

At about four o'clock in the afternoon the phone in my office rang. Our friend Kathy was on the other end of the line. "Our house was just hit by a tornado," she said. At first I thought she was using a metaphor, like when your house is a mess and you say it looks like a tornado has been through it. But I quickly realized this was not the voice of someone joking. Their house had literally been hit by a tornado.

I jumped into the car and headed as fast as I could safely go to their neighborhood. As I drove, I tried to prepare myself mentally for what I would see. I had seen a lot of pictures and heard a lot of descriptions about the impact of tornadoes. Yet the thought of my friend's house being destroyed seemed unreal. Coming closer I began to hear sirens blaring. I scanned the neighborhoods trying to spot any sign of the damage, but everything looked normal.

Finally coming within two or three blocks of their house, I could go no farther by car because police had already sealed off the affected area. I hastily parked my car along the street, jumped out, and began running toward my friend's house. As I came up the street and crested a small hill, I suddenly stopped dead in my tracks. I could hardly believe my eyes. I thought I understood what tornado damage would look like, but I was honestly not prepared for what I was witnessing now. Immediately all the ways people had tried to describe to me the effects of a tornado made perfect sense. I now understood tornadoes in a way I never had before.

Now I never really doubted what people told me. I tried to imagine what they meant when they said it was like a bomb going off: finely ground pieces of everything scattered all over, the ground now just mud because the grass had been literally pulled from its roots, insulation fibers coating everything. I had heard those kinds of stories before, but seeing was truly believing. Somehow witnessing it with my own eyes gave it credibility, a *realness* that it had never had before.

"Seeing is believing." How many times have we heard that phrase? It's almost an axiom by which we modern people live. In our scientific and technological age we want everything to be validated by empirical evidence. We don't like to take somebody's word for it; we want proof. As we have come toward another celebration of Easter and consider the story of what happened on Easter Day, we are being asked to believe the most amazing event ever—that a man who was crucified, stone cold dead, and buried could be resurrected from the dead. What would it take for you to believe that such a thing could happen? How about if you saw it with your own eyes? That would just about do away with any doubt, wouldn't it? Well, in this passage John seems to have something to say to us about that.

There is a sense in which John's entire Gospel is about seeing and believing. The question John seems most interested in is simple: "What does it mean to believe?" Throughout this Gospel there are many reports of people seeing with their own eyes who Jesus really is. They did witness some amazing things. They saw sight restored to the blind and lame people walking again; they even saw a dead man raised to life. Plus, they heard remarkable teaching.

It would seem reasonable that being this *hands-on* with Jesus would produce faith every time. It did not. John makes it clear in his telling of the story that when some people saw Jesus' miraculous signs and heard his teaching, they had faith in him as the Son of God. But John makes it equally clear that some others, even though they saw and heard the same things, did not believe. Perhaps it is possible to see and yet not really see. Perhaps seeing is not necessarily believing.

In this story are three different responses to seeing the same thing. The highlight of the story seems to be in verse 8 when John finally follows Peter into the empty tomb, sees the grave clothes lying there, and believes. Perhaps we think, *Well of course, if I could see that kind of evidence I would easily believe.* But notice that Mary Magdalene also saw the empty tomb and her conclusion was that grave robbers had been there. Peter rushed into the tomb ahead of John and didn't understand what was going on. And even though the text says of John, "He saw and believed," it is interesting that only a few paragraphs later John will be huddled with the other disciples behind locked doors in fear because they still don't know what is happening.

Even though these people had all witnessed the empty tomb, it really didn't change their lives much. It would not be long before they go back to fishing. They certainly believed the tomb was empty; they saw it. But what did they really understand about resurrection? Could it be that this is the key question for Easter Day? What does it mean to *believe* in the resurrection of Jesus? It is one thing to see, it is another thing to believe, and it is still another thing to understand. There is a big difference between believing that something happened once upon a time and believing that Jesus is alive now and is present with us.

The truth is, it was the *presence* of Jesus that made all the difference for these disciples. They saw with their own eyes that the tomb was empty, but apparently that alone was not enough. It was not until later when Jesus appears to them and spends time with them that they really come to understand what resurrection means. If we say, "Oh yes, I believe in Jesus; I believe in Easter," yet it does not make a significant difference in our lives, then we do not really believe. The kind of belief or faith that John is calling us to is entering into a relationship with a living Christ. This is where our lives are changed. This is where Jesus makes a real difference in the way we live.

Seeing with our *eyes* has never been the point of Christian faith. Seeing with our *heart* always has been. If you intellectually affirm the story of the Gospel, that Jesus lived, died, and rose again, this is good. However, the central question is, "Does it make any difference in your life?" The belief that I live every day in the presence of Jesus Christ who is alive gives me hope when nothing else in my life does. And when you really believe in the resurrection, then you are a possessor of real life even when everything else around you screams death.

So the question today is, "Do you believe?" This is more than a matter of seeing or somehow having it proved. Authentic belief moves from head to heart. This is about opening your heart to the presence of Jesus who will, by his Spirit, take up residence in your heart to bring forgiveness, peace, and a sure hope. —JR

After reading the passage from John 20:1-18
and the devotional reflection "Do You Believe?"
you may also want to read the
following related passages:
Acts 10:34-43; Psalm 118:1-2, 14-24; Colossians 3:1-4

The discussion prompts that follow will help prepare you to participate in your Sunday school class or small-group study. Use your reflective journaling section to record any other insights that come to you as you read the Gospel lesson and the devotional reflection.

DISCUSSION PROMPT #1: JOHN 20

For Peter and John in this resurrection account, in contrast to Mary's experience, there were no angels, no reassuring words, and no appearance of the risen Jesus. Instead, they see only the evidence of empty grave clothes lying in an empty tomb. Which experience, for you, would be more convincing that Jesus has risen from the dead?

DISCUSSION PROMPT #2: JOHN 20

Over 2,000 years later, what evidence do we have that Jesus' resurrection occurred?

DISCUSSION PROMPT #3: JOHN 20

In light of the message Jesus tells Mary to deliver to the disciples (v. 17), do you think he is talking more about his relationship with God the Father or our relationship with God? Explain.

DISCUSSION PROMPT #4: DEVOTIONAL REFLECTION

What part of this resurrection account makes the deepest emotional impact on you? What does the devotional writer mean by the statement, "Authentic belief moves from head to heart?"

REFLECTIVE JOURNALING

_____

_____

_____

_____

_____

_____

_____

_____

_____

_____

_____

_____

_____

_____

_____

_____

_____

_____

_____

_____

_____

_____

_____

_____

_____

PSALM 98 ▪ JONAH 2:1-9 ▪ ACTS 2:14, 22-32 ▪ JOHN 14:1-14

MORNING MEDITATIONS

PRAYER—O God, you are the giver of all good gifts and I desire to praise your name for all of your goodness to me. I thank you for sending your Son to die for my sins, for the means of grace, and for the hope of glory, through Jesus Christ. Amen. **JW**

PSALM 98:1, 3b—O sing to the Lord a new song, for he has done marvelous thins. His right hand and his holy arm have gotten him the victory . . . All the ends of the earth have seen the victory of our God.

JONAH 2:2a, 3a, 7ab, 9b   *Deliverance Belongs to the Lord*
Jonah prayed . . . , "I called to the Lord out of my distress and he answered me . . . You cast me into the deep . . . As my life was ebbing away, I remembered the Lord; and my prayer came to you . . . deliverance belongs to the Lord."

ACTS 2:31-32   *He Was Not Abandoned*
David spoke of the resurrection of the Messiah, saying, "He was not abandoned to Hades, nor did his flesh experience corruption." This Jesus God raised up, and of that all of us are witnesses.

JOHN 14:1-14   *Today's Gospel Reading*

I am the Christ. It is I who destroyed death, who triumphed over the enemy, who trampled hell underfoot, who bound the strong one and snatched many away to the heights of heaven. I am the Christ.   FROM A SERMON BY MELITO OF SARDIS

EVENING REFLECTIONS

PSALM 66:5, 8b-9, 19—Come and see what God has done; he is awesome in his deeds among mortals . . . Let the sound of his praise be heard, who has kept us among the living and has not let our feet slip. Truly God has listened . . . to the words of my prayer.

PRAYER—Lord, now that we have come to the setting of the sun and see the evening light, we give praise to God: Father, Son and Holy Spirit. Worthy are you at all times to be worshipped with holy voices, O Risen Christ and giver of life; therefore the world glorifies you. Amen.

PSALM 103 ▪ ISAIAH 30:18-21 ▪ ACTS 2:36-41 ▪ JOHN 14:15-31

MORNING MEDITATIONS

PRAYER—O Lord, you did not please yourself even though all things were created for your pleasure. Let some portion of your Spirit descend on me, so that I may deny myself and follow you, in Jesus' name, Amen. **JW**

PSALM 103:1, 4b-5, 19, 22b—Bless the LORD, O my soul, and all that is within me, bless his holy name . . . The LORD has established his throne in the heavens, and his kingdom rules over all. . . . Bless the LORD, O my soul.

ISAIAH 30:18 *The Lord Waits to Be Gracious to You*
Therefore the LORD waits to be gracious to you; therefore he will rise up to show mercy to you. For the LORD is a God of justice; blessed are all those who wait for him.

ACTS 2:36, 38 *God Has Made Jesus Lord and Messiah*
Therefore let the entire house of Israel know with certainty that God has made him both Lord and Messiah, this Jesus whom you crucified . . . Repent, and be baptized every one of you in the name of Jesus Christ so that your sins may be forgiven; and you will receive the gift of the Holy Spirit.

JOHN 14:15-31 *Today's Gospel Reading*

Sacred scripture had foretold from the beginning Christ's death and the sufferings which preceded his death. But it also proclaims what happened to his dead body after his death, and declares that the God to whom this happened is impassible and immortal.

A READING FROM A SERMON BY ANASTASIUS OF ANTIOCH

EVENING REFLECTIONS

PSALM 111:2a, 9-10—Great are the works of the LORD . . . He sent redemption to his people . . . Holy and awesome is his name. The fear of the LORD is the beginning of wisdom; all those who practice it have a good understanding. His praise endures forever.

PRAYER—O Lamb of God, give me grace throughout my whole life, in every thought, and word and work, to imitate your meekness and humility. May I go through all the scenes of life not seeking my own glory, but looking wholly unto you, and acting wholly for you, through Christ my Lord. Amen. **JW**

PSALM 97 ▪ MICAH 7:7-15 ▪ ACTS 3:1-10 ▪ JOHN 15:1-11

MORNING MEDITATIONS

PRAYER—O Lord, you have set before us the great hope that your kingdom shall come on earth, and have taught us to pray for its coming; give us grace to discern the signs of its dawning, and to work for the perfect day when your will shall be done on earth as it is in heaven, in the name of Jesus, I pray. Amen. **JW**

PSALM 97:1a, **6, 11**—The LORD is king! Let the earth rejoice . . . The heavens proclaim his righteousness; and all the people behold his glory . . . Light dawns for the righteous, and joy for the upright in heart.

MICAH 7:7, 9d *I Will Look to the Lord*
But as for me, I will look to the LORD, I will wait for the God of my salvation; my God will hear me . . . He will bring me to the light; I shall see his vindication.

ACTS 3:6-8 *What I Have, I Give*
Peter said, "I have no silver or gold, but what I have I give you; in the name of Jesus Christ of Nazareth, stand up and walk." And he took him by the right hand and raised him up . . . He stood and began to walk, and he entered the temple with them, walking and leaping and praising God.

JOHN 15:1-11 *Today's Gospel Reading*

Thus the passion of the Savior is salvation for all humankind. This was why he willed to die for us, that we should believe in him, and live forever. He willed to become for a time what we are, so that we should receive the promise of his eternity and live with him forever. A READING FROM AN ANCIENT HOMILY

EVENING REFLECTIONS

PSALM 115:1, 12a, 13—Not to us, O LORD, not to us, but to your name give glory, for the sake of your steadfast love and your faithfulness . . . The LORD has been mindful of us; he will bless us . . . he will bless those who fear the LORD, both small and great.

PRAYER—O Lord, visit this place we pray, and drive far from it all the snares of the enemy; may your holy angels dwell with us and guard us in peace, and may your blessings be upon us evermore; through Jesus Christ, our Lord. Amen.

PSALM 146 ▪ EZEKIEL 37:1-14 ▪ ACTS 3:11-26 ▪ JOHN 15:12-27

MORNING MEDITATIONS

PRAYER—Eternal God, my Sovereign Lord, I acknowledge all I am, all I have is yours. I humbly thank you for all the blessings you have bestowed upon me—for creating me in your own image, for redeeming me by the death of your blessed Son, and for the assistance of the Holy Spirit, through Christ I pray. Amen. *JW*

PSALM 146:7c-8, 10—The LORD sets the prisoners free; the LORD opens the eyes of the blind. The LORD lifts up those who are bowed down; the LORD loves the righteous . . . The LORD will reign forever, your God, O Zion, for all generations. Praise the LORD!

EZEKIEL 37:13-14a   *I Will Open Your Graves*
And you shall know that I am the LORD, when I open your graves, and bring you up from your graves, O my people. I will put my spirit within you, and you shall live.

ACTS 3:13, 19-20   *Turn to God*
The God of Abraham, Isaac and Jacob, the God of our ancestors has glorified his servant Jesus, whom you handed over and rejected in the presence of Pilate . . . Repent therefore, and turn to God so that your sins may be wiped out, so that times of refreshing may come from the presence of the Lord.

JOHN 15:12-27   *Today's Gospel Reading*

What boundless love! The innocent hands and feet of Christ were pierced by the nails: he suffered the pain. I suffer neither pain nor anguish, yet by letting me participate in his pain, he gives me the free gift of salvation.
                    A READING FROM INSTRUCTIONS TO NEWLY BAPTIZED CHRISTIANS IN JERUSALEM

EVENING REFLECTIONS

PSALM 148:1-2, 13—Praise the LORD! Praise the LORD from the heavens; praise him in the heights! Praise him, all his angels; praise him, all his host! . . . Let them praise the name of the LORD, for his name alone is exalted; his glory is above earth and heaven.

PRAYER—O God, as darkness falls you renew your promise to reveal the light of your presence. May your Word be a lantern to my feet and a light unto my path that I may walk as a child of light and sing your praise throughout the world, in Jesus' name. Amen

PSALM 136 ▪ DANIEL 12:1-4, 13 ▪ ACTS 4:1-12 ▪ JOHN 16:1-15

MORNING MEDITATIONS

PRAYER—Almighty God, I bless you from my heart. O Savior of the World, God of God, Light of Light, you have destroyed the power of the devil, you have overcome death, and you sit at the right hand of the Father. Be today my light and peace and make me a new creature, through Christ my Lord. Amen. *JW*

PSALM 136:1-2, 23a, 24a—O give thanks to the Lord, for he is good, for his steadfast love endures forever. O give thanks to the God of gods, for his steadfast love endures forever . . . It is he who remembered us in our low estate . . . and rescued us from our foes.

DANIEL 12:2-3 *Shining like Stars*
Many of those who sleep in the dust of the earth shall awake, some to everlasting life and some to shame and everlasting contempt. Those who are wise shall shine like the brightness of the sky, and those who lead many to righteousness, like the stars forever and ever.

ACTS 4:8b, 10 *By the Name of Jesus*
Rulers of the people and elders . . . let it be known to all of you . . . that this man is standing before you in good health by the name of Jesus Christ of Nazareth whom you crucified, whom God raised from the dead.

JOHN 16:1-15 *Today's Gospel Reading*

This is the day which the Lord has made. Let us be glad and rejoice in it. What is this day? It is he who is the source of life . . . the author of life—our Lord Jesus Christ, who said of himself, "I am the day; he who walks by daylight does not stumble."

A READING FROM AN ANCIENT EASTER SERMON

EVENING REFLECTIONS

PSALM 118:7, 15a, 17—The Lord is on my side to help me; I shall look in triumph on those who hate me . . . There are glad songs of victory in the tents of the righteous . . . I shall not die but live, and recount the deeds of the Lord.

PRAYER—O Lord, I give you my entire liberty, my memory, my understanding and my whole will. All that I am and all that I possess you have given me: I surrender it all to you to be disposed of according to your will. Give me only your love and your grace; with these I will be rich enough and desire nothing more. Amen. *JW*

PSALM 145 ▪ ISAIAH 25:1-9 ▪ ACTS 4:13-31 ▪ JOHN 16:16-33

MORNING MEDITATIONS

PRAYER—Lord of all life and power, through the mighty resurrection of Jesus, you have overcome sin and death to make all things new in him. This is the day you have made; I will rejoice and be glad in it. Amen.

PSALM 145:10-11, 13a-b—All your works shall give thanks to you, O Lord, and all your faithful shall bless you. They shall speak of the glory of your kingdom, and tell of your power . . . Your kingdom is an everlasting kingdom, and your dominion endures throughout all generations.

ISAIAH 25:6a, 7-8a, 9a   *He Will Swallow Up Death*
On this mountain the Lord of hosts will make for all peoples a feast of . . . rich food . . . and he will destroy on this mountain the shroud that is cast over all peoples, the sheet that is spread over all nations; he will swallow up death forever. . . . It will be said on that day, Lo, this is our God.

ACTS 4:29-30   *Let Me Speak Boldly*
And now, Lord . . . grant to your servants to speak your word with all boldness, while you stretch out your hand to heal, and signs and wonders are performed through the name of your holy servant Jesus.

JOHN 16:16-33   *Today's Gospel Reading*

Now you walk by faith, as long as you journey in this mortal body far from the Lord. But Jesus Christ towards whom you are moving is a sure way. He is this in his humanity which he took on for us. He has in reserve an abundance of grace for those who reverence him.

A READING FROM A SERMON BY ST. AUGUSTINE

EVENING REFLECTIONS

PSALM 104:1-2a, 34—Bless the Lord, O my soul. O Lord my God, you are very great. You are clothed with honor and majesty, wrapped in light as with a garment . . . May my meditation be pleasing to him, for I rejoice in the Lord.

PRAYER—Now to God the Father who first loved us and made us accepted in the Beloved; to God the Son who loved us and washed us from our sins in his own blood; to God the Holy Spirit who sheds the love of God abroad in our hearts, be all love and all glory for time and for eternity. Amen. *JW*

WEEK TWO
EASTER SEASON

Ashes to Fire Week 8

Sunday: With Jesus Behind Locked Doors

Read the Gospel passage from John 20:19-31, the devotional reflection titled "Putting Faith in Your Doubts," and respond to the discussion prompts in the Reflective Journaling section.

THE MUSIC OF ASHES TO FIRE

Week 8: "Open" (Track 9)

Monday through Saturday of Easter Season Week 2

IN THE MORNING:

A personal daily devotional guide includes prayer, a reading from the Old Testament, the Psalms, the Epistles, and the Gospel for each day of the week.

This week's readings are from Daniel, 1 John, and the Gospel of Luke.

Inspirational quotes from men and women of faith keep us in contact with our shared Christian heritage.

IN THE EVENING:

An evening psalm and prayer become preludes to nighttime rest and renewal.

EASTER SEASON—WEEK TWO
With Jesus Behind Locked Doors

A devotional reflection based on John 20:19-31

Read the Gospel passage first, then the devotional reflection that follows. The discussion prompts at the end will help prepare you for Sunday school and small-group sessions.

Putting Faith in Your Doubts

Most of life has to be sorted out, not in a church service or a classroom or even at the family table, but "out there" where opinions intersect and values clash, where traditions are challenged and messages get compromised. It is in the living of life that truth finally gets firmly pressed into a person's character by the hammer and anvil of faith and doubt.

In many ways, doubt is an important part of faith. It is often a signpost, marking the pathway to faith. It is natural for believers to resist the presence and pull of doubt, and yet faith need not be blind faith—for there is such a thing as honest doubt. There are moments when we feel like questioning God.

How can this be?

What does this mean?

Why me?

The Bible is filled with such questions, many of them directed toward God. Jesus at the point of his own death cried out, "My God, my God, why have you forsaken me?" Questions can be helpful, for they have a way of giving voice to our doubts and once we acknowledge such things we can deal with them.

Perhaps there is no other story in the Bible that helps us understand doubt and faith quite like the story of doubting Thomas. To really hear what the stories of the Bible are saying we must hear them as stories about ourselves. For example, it is not until you see yourself in the story of the prodigal son (or daughter) that you grasp what forgiveness and acceptance really feel like. Thus, to grasp the interplay of faith and doubt more fully, a person needs to see himself or herself in this story from John 20.

Following the death of Jesus, the frightened and bewildered disciples were gathered behind locked doors, stunned by the events of the past few days. John tells us that suddenly "Jesus came and stood among them and said, 'Peace be with you.'" Jesus showed the group his hands and side. It was then they recognized him.

However, one of the disciples was missing. That was Thomas. Thomas was a cautious man—the kind of fellow who would wear both a belt and suspenders. He took no chances. As far as Thomas was concerned, Jesus was dead and that was the end of it.

Thomas was aware that Mary Magdalene claimed that she had seen Jesus, and he heard that the others were claiming the same thing—but Thomas had not seen him and declared, "Unless I see the nail marks in his hands and put my finger where the nails were, and put my hand into his side, I will not believe it."

If Thomas had been born and raised in America, he would have come from Missouri, the Show-Me State. For him, seeing was believing.

There are many moments in the journey of life when we may find ourselves at the intersection of faith and doubt. The resurrection of Jesus is certainly one such place—but there are others. Does God exist at all? If he does exist, can we know him personally or is God a distant being who, having created the world and set its laws in motion, took a seat on the sidelines to watch and perhaps even wonder about what would happen next.

What about miracles or prayer? How do we reconcile suffering with the image of a loving and all-powerful God? There is legitimate room for doubt—but Easter declares that there is more room for faith!

Some have noted that doubt can be seen as a necessary element of genuine faith. Can you have light without shadow? Perhaps having room for doubt is what makes trusting possible.

Yet, even so, we want to know for sure. *"Lord, let me see a burning bush or let the Chicago Cubs win the pennant—then I will believe in miracles. Then I will know for sure there is a God!"* But this business of knowing for sure might change our relationship with God.

God's creative design is not for us as humans to be robots—but to be free, loving beings. With freedom comes risk, the risk that some might use their freedom to say no to God. Yet, even then, God provided for reconciliation through Jesus. God doesn't force us to believe—he invites us and loves us into belief. That's what he did for Thomas.

How does a person move from doubt to faith? In response to Thomas's affirmation comes what is perhaps the most salient part of the conversation. Jesus said, "Because you have seen me, you have believed; blessed are those who have not seen and yet have believed."

In that statement Jesus had us in mind. We have not seen him with our eyes or touched the nail-scarred hands. Nonetheless, we can see him with our hearts and spirits. We can know. It is not with the eyes of our head that we know certain things. Can you see love? Can you see sound or taste?

"Faith . . . is the evidence of things not seen" (Hebrews 11:1, KJV). As we believe . . . we can see the risen Savior, and in so doing we make room for faith in our doubts. —JB

After reading the passage from John 20:19-31 and the devotional reflection "Putting Faith in Your Doubts" you may also want to read:
Acts 2:14a, 22-32; Psalm 16; 1 Peter 1:3-9

The **discussion prompts** that follow will help prepare you to participate in your Sunday school class or small-group study. Use your **reflective journaling** section to record any other insights that come to you as you read the Gospel lesson and the devotional reflection.

DISCUSSION PROMPT #1: JOHN 20
Thomas insisted that he needed evidence before he would believe Jesus had risen. What evidence can we show someone like Thomas today that Jesus is alive?

DISCUSSION PROMPT #2: DEVOTIONAL REFLECTION
The author of the devotional reflection writes: "Some have noted that doubt can be seen as a necessary element of genuine faith." What does the writer mean by that statement?

DISCUSSION PROMPT #3: JOHN 20
Verse 22 reads, "He breathed on them and said . . . 'Receive the Holy Spirit.'" What do these words mean for the disciples? For us? Compare with Genesis 2:7.

DISCUSSION PROMPT #4: JOHN 20

Using your imagination, what "other signs" (v. 30) could Jesus have done that John did not write about that might bolster your faith?

REFLECTIVE JOURNALING

_____

_____

_____

_____

_____

_____

_____

_____

_____

_____

_____

_____

_____

_____

_____

_____

_____

_____

_____

_____

_____

_____

PSALM 3 ▪ DANIEL 1:1-21 ▪ 1 JOHN 1:1-10 ▪ JOHN 17:1-11

MORNING MEDITATIONS

PRAYER—O God, you are the giver of all good gifts and I desire to praise your name for all of your goodness to me. I thank you for sending your Son to die for my sins, for the means of grace, and for the hope of glory, through Jesus Christ. Amen. **JW**

PSALM 3:3, 7a, 8—But you, O Lord, are a shield around me, my glory, and the one who lifts up my head . . . Rise up, O Lord! Deliver me, O my God . . . Deliverance belongs to the Lord; may your blessing be on your people!

DANIEL 1:8, 12, 15, 17   *Keep Yourself Pure*
Daniel resolved that he would not defile himself with the royal rations of food . . . "Please test your servants for ten days. Let us be given vegetables to eat and water to drink" . . . At the end of ten days it was observed that they appeared better than the young men who had been eating the royal rations. . . . To these four young men God gave knowledge and skill . . . and wisdom.

1 JOHN 1:1-2   *The Word of Life*
We declare to you what was from the beginning . . . what we have . . . touched with our hands, concerning the word of life . . . and we . . . declare to you the eternal life that was with the Father and was revealed to us.

JOHN 17:1-11   *Today's Gospel Reading*

Unique. Absolute. Perfect. Those infinities Jesus claims; and these make Deity. Nothing here of the "finite God." Let the mind reel, understand it or not, Jesus demands a reckless faith . . . His life and his words prove him true. None but God could have conceived such a life and such words.   FROM BERTHA MUNRO, *TRUTH FOR TODAY*

EVENING REFLECTIONS

PSALM 4:8—I will both lie down and sleep in peace; for you alone, O Lord, make me lie down in safety.

PRAYER—O God, fill my soul with so entire a love for you, that I may love nothing but you. Give me grace to study your knowledge daily, that the more I know you, the more I may love you, through Jesus Christ my Lord. Amen. **JW**

PSALM 5 ▪ DANIEL 2:1-23 ▪ 1 JOHN 2:1-11 ▪ JOHN 17:12-19

MORNING MEDITATIONS

PRAYER—Lord of all life and power, through the mighty resurrection of Jesus, you have overcome sin and death to make all things new in him. This is the day you have made; I will rejoice and be glad in it. Amen.

PSALM 5:3, 7-8a—O Lord, in the morning you hear my voice; in the morning I plead my case to you, and wait . . . But I, through the abundance of your steadfast love . . . will bow down toward your temple in awe of you. Lead me, Lord, in your righteousness.

DANIEL 2:20-21 *Wisdom Belongs to God*
Blessed be the name of God from age to age, for wisdom and power are his. He changes times and seasons, deposes kings and sets up kings; he gives wisdom to the wise and knowledge to those who have understanding.

1 JOHN 2:1b-2 *We Have an Advocate*
If anyone does sin, we have an advocate with the Father, Jesus Christ the righteous, and he is the atoning sacrifice for our sins, and not for ours only but also for the sins of the whole world.

JOHN 17:12-19 *Today's Gospel Reading*

Glory to you! You built your cross as a bridge over death, so that souls might pass from the realm of death to the realm of life . . . You put on the body of a mortal man and made it the source of life for all mortal men. You are alive!

AN EXCERPT FROM A SERMON BY EPHRAEM

EVENING REFLECTIONS

PSALM 11:4-5a, 7—The Lord is in his holy temple . . . His eyes behold, his gaze examines humankind. The Lord tests the righteous . . . For the Lord is righteous; he loves righteous deeds; the upright behold his face.

PRAYER—O Lamb of God, give me grace throughout my whole life, in every thought, and word and work, to imitate your meekness and humility. May I go through all the scenes of life not seeking my own glory, but looking wholly unto you, and acting wholly for you, through Christ my Lord. Amen. **JW**

PSALM 119:1-24 ▪ DANIEL 2:17-30 ▪ 1 JOHN 2:1-11 ▪ JOHN 17:20-26

MORNING MEDITATIONS

PRAYER—Lord God, send your Holy Spirit to be the guide of all my ways, and the sanctifier of my soul and body. Give me the light of your presence, your peace from heaven, and the salvation of my soul, through Jesus Christ my Lord. Amen. *JW*

PSALM 119:10-11—With my whole heart I seek you; do not let me stray from your commandments. I treasure your word in my heart, so that I may not sin against you.

DANIEL 2:22-23b *Light Dwells with Him*
He reveals deep and hidden things; he knows what is in the darkness, and light dwells with him. To you, O God of my ancestors, I give thanks and praise, for you have given me wisdom and power.

1 JOHN 2:7ab, 10 *An Old Commandment*
Beloved, I am writing you no new commandment, but an old commandment that you have heard from the beginning . . . Whoever loves a brother or sister lives in the light, and in such a person there is no cause for stumbling.

JOHN 17:20-26 *Today's Gospel Reading*

For while God preserves in the Church his love, which is poured out through the Holy Spirit, he makes the Church a sacrifice pleasing to himself, so that she may always be able to receive the grace of spiritual love and so continuously offer herself as a living and holy sacrifice.   A QUOTE FROM FULGENTIUS OF RUSUPE

EVENING REFLECTIONS

PSALM 13:3, 5—Consider and answer me, O Lᴏʀᴅ my God! Give light to my eyes, or I will sleep the sleep of death . . . I trusted in your steadfast love; my heart shall rejoice in your salvation.

PRAYER—Father, grant me forgiveness of what is past, that in the days to come I may with a pure spirit do your will—walking humbly with you, showing love to all, and keeping body and soul in sanctification and honor, in Jesus' name. Amen. *JW*

PSALM 18:1-20 ▪ DANIEL 2:31-49 ▪ 1 JOHN 2:15-29 ▪ LUKE 3:1-14

MORNING MEDITATIONS

PRAYER—Eternal God, my Sovereign Lord, I acknowledge all I am, all I have is yours. I humbly thank you for all the blessings you have bestowed upon me—for creating me in your own image, for redeeming me by the death of your blessed Son, and for the assistance of the Holy Spirit, through Christ I pray. Amen. **JW**

PSALM 18: 1, 16-17a, 19—I love you, O Lᴏʀᴅ, my strength . . . He reached down from on high, he took me; he drew me out of mighty waters, He delivered me from my strong enemy. . . . He brought me out to a broad place; he delivered me, because he delighted in me.

DANIEL 2:47-48 *Truly, God Is God*
The king said to Daniel, "Truly, your God is God of gods and Lord of kings and a revealer of mysteries, for you have been able to reveal this mystery!" Then the king promoted Daniel, gave him many great gifts, and made him ruler over the whole province of Babylon.

1 JOHN 2:15, 17 *The World Is Passing Away*
Do not love the world or the things in the world. The love of the Father is not in those who love the world . . . the world and its desires are passing away, but those who do the will of God live forever.

LUKE 3:1-14 *Today's Gospel Reading*

Meister Eckhart wrote: "There are plenty to follow our Lord half-way, but not the other half. They will give up possessions, friends and honors, but it touches them too closely to disown themselves." It is just this astonishing life which is willing to follow him the other half . . . I propose to you.   FROM THOMAS KELLY, *A TESTAMENT OF DEVOTION*

EVENING REFLECTIONS

PSALM 18:31-32, 50—For who is God except the Lᴏʀᴅ? And who is a rock besides our God?—the God who girded me with strength, and made my way safe . . . Great triumphs he gives to his king, and shows steadfast love to his anointed.

PRAYER—To you, O God, Father, Son, and Holy Spirit, my Creator, Redeemer, and Sanctifier, I give up myself entirely; may I no longer serve myself, but you only, all the days of my life, through Christ my Lord, I pray. Amen. **JW**

PSALM 16 ▪ **DANIEL 3:1-18** ▪ **1 JOHN 3:1-10** ▪ **LUKE 3:15-22**

MORNING MEDITATIONS

PRAYER—Lord of all life and power, through the mighty resurrection of Jesus, you have overcome sin and death to make all things new in him. This is the day you have made; I will rejoice and be glad in it. Amen.

PSALM 16:5a, 6, 11—The LORD is my chosen portion and my cup . . . the boundary lines have fallen for me in pleasant places; I have a goodly heritage . . . You show me the path of life, in your presence there is fullness of joy; in your right hand are pleasures forevermore.

DANIEL 3:16b-18a   *We Will Not Bow Down*
O Nebuchadnezzar, we have no need to present a defense to you in this matter. If our God whom we serve is able to deliver us from the furnace of blazing fire and out of your hand, O king, let him deliver us. But if not, be it known to you, O king, that we will not serve your gods.

1 JOHN 3:2b-3   *We Will Be like Him*
What we do know is this: when he is revealed, we will be like him, for we will see him as he is. All who have this hope in him purify themselves, just as he is pure.

LUKE 3:15-22   *Today's Gospel Reading*

When Christians say the Christ-life is in them, they do not mean simply something mental or moral . . . They mean that Christ is actually operating through them; the whole mass of Christians are the physical organism through which Christ acts.

FROM C. S. LEWIS, *MERE CHRISTIANITY*

EVENING REFLECTIONS

PSALM 135:5, 13—For I know that the LORD is great; our Lord is above all gods . . . Your name, O LORD, endures forever; your renown, O LORD, throughout all ages.

PRAYER—Father, accept my imperfect repentance, show compassion for my infirmities, forgive my faults, purify my motives, strengthen my weakness, and let your good Spirit watch over me, and your love ever rule my heart, through the mercies of Jesus, I pray. Amen. *JW*

PSALM 21:1-7 ▪ DANIEL 3:19-30 ▪ 1 JOHN 3:11-18 ▪ LUKE 4:1-13

MORNING MEDITATIONS

PRAYER—Lord of all life and power, you have destroyed death through the resurrection of your Son Jesus Christ. I pray today that I may live in his presence and rejoice in the hope of eternal glory; through Jesus Christ, to whom with you and the Holy Spirit, be dominion and praise for ever and ever. Amen.

PSALM 21:1, 3-4—In your strength the king rejoices . . . and in your help how greatly he exults . . . For you meet him with rich blessings; you set a crown of fine gold on his head. He asked you for life; you gave it to him—length of days forever and ever.

DANIEL 3:24-25   *The Fourth Man*
Then King Nebuchadnezzar was astonished . . . "Was it not three men that we threw bound into the fire? . . . But I see four men unbound . . . and they are not hurt; and the fourth has the appearance of a god.

1 JOHN 3:13-14a, 16a   *He Laid Down His Life for Us*
Do not be astonished, brothers and sisters, that the world hates you. We know that we have passed from death to life because we love one another . . . We know love by this, that he laid down his life for us.

LUKE 4:1-13   *Today's Gospel Reading*

The Lord, to prepare us for the risen life, lays before us all the gospel precepts . . . We must avoid anger, endure evil, be free from the love of money. So shall we by our own choice achieve those things which are natural endowments of the world to come.

FROM A TREATISE *ON THE HOLY SPIRIT* BY BASIL THE GREAT

EVENING REFLECTIONS

PSALM 116:8-10a, 17—For you have delivered my soul from death, my eyes from tears, my feet from stumbling. I walk before the Lord in the land of the living. I kept my faith . . . I will offer to you a thanksgiving sacrifice and call on the name of the Lord.

PRAYER—Now to God the Father who first loved us and made us accepted in the Beloved; to God the Son who loved us and washed us from our sins in his own blood; to God the Holy Spirit who sheds the love of God abroad in our hearts, be all love and all glory for time and for eternity. Amen. **JW**

WEEK THREE
EASTER SEASON

Ashes to Fire Week 9

Sunday: With Jesus at a Supper Table

Read the Gospel passage from Luke 24:13-35, the devotional reflection titled "Sunset, Sunrise," and respond to the discussion prompts in the Reflective Journaling section.

THE MUSIC OF ASHES TO FIRE

Week 9: "Remember and Proclaim" (Track 10)

Monday through Saturday of Easter Season Week 3

IN THE MORNING:

A personal daily devotional guide includes prayer, a reading from the Old Testament, the Psalms, the Epistles, and the Gospel for each day of the week.

This week's readings are from Daniel, 1, 2, and 3 John, and the Gospel of Luke.

Inspirational quotes from men and women of faith keep us in contact with our shared Christian heritage.

IN THE EVENING:

An evening psalm and prayer become preludes to nighttime rest and renewal.

EASTER SEASON–WEEK THREE
With Jesus at a Supper Table

A devotional reflection based on Luke 24:13-35

Read the Gospel passage first, then the devotional reflection that follows. The discussion prompts at the end will help prepare you for Sunday school and small-group sessions.

Sunset, Sunrise

Easter is not an argument; it is an affirmation. It is an announcement of the faith that overcomes the world. It is a declaration of the truth that light triumphs over darkness. Lilies do not argue that spring is here; they simply bloom and thus declare it so. Just so, Easter is an announcement that light is stronger than darkness, that life is more powerful than death, that hope is greater than despair, and that victory belongs to heaven rather than to earth.

Luke tells the poignant story of two disciples who begin walking sadly into the sunset but who conclude by running headlong into the sunrise. It was late on the afternoon of the first day of the week following the crucifixion of Jesus. Forty-eight hours had passed since his death. These disciples had stayed in Jerusalem two full days and had been part of the huddled fellowship of followers trying to make sense of what had happened. Finally they decided to leave Jerusalem and their buried hopes behind.

They headed out of the city, walking the road to Emmaus, a small town about seven miles west of Jerusalem. Because they were walking due west, they were headed into the sunset. And that was somehow very appropriate, because their spirits were sinking as well. Their grief was great, for the One they had believed to be the Messiah had been stripped, beaten, humiliated, and put to death on a cross. For these disciples the light had gone out. All about them they saw only sunset and the coming darkness.

As these two walked into the deepening shadows, caught up in their own conversation about the events of the past few days, they were joined by a third person. It is difficult to say exactly why—perhaps it was the sun in their eyes, the distraction of their own conversation, the weight of their grief, or more likely the Holy Spirit, who veiled their discernment—but for whatever reason they did not recognize that this third person was Jesus.

What a wonderful thought—the One for whom they mourned was walking in their midst. The hope they had given up was present beside them.

Years ago a man named C. M. Sheldon wrote a book titled *Jesus Is Here*, in which he tells a series of fictitious stories about individuals who at times of great distress experienced the presence of Christ in their lives:

- a surgeon who was about to operate on a terribly injured accident victim only to discover that the victim was his estranged son
- a timid girl whose mean-spirited mother attacked and belittled her daily

These individuals and others, bullied, baffled, or simply buffeted about by the circumstances of life in Sheldon's stories, were all visited by a present and living Christ. Although the stories in his book were fictitious, the truth toward which the stories move is undeniable and has been validated by many believers across the centuries, beginning with the two who were headed toward Emmaus.

As Jesus began to walk with these two downcast disciples he asked, "What are you discussing together as you walk along?" In response they pour out their hearts to him about the events of the past few days. "We had hoped that he was the one who was going to redeem Israel," they said. But now he was gone.

Jesus listened and then answered them, and as he did, their sunset began to turn to sunrise. "Did not the Christ have to suffer these things and then enter his glory?" Jesus asked. Then beginning with Moses and all the prophets he explained what the Scriptures said concerning these events.

As the travelers approached the village, it appeared that Jesus would go on, but the two asked him to stay saying, "Stay with us, for it is nearly evening; the day is almost over." So Jesus stayed.

Jesus will always stay if we will invite him to do so. He will enter any life, any home, any circumstance if we will only ask. John records this promise in Revelation 3:20, "Here I am! I stand at the door and knock. If anyone hears my voice and opens the door, I will come in and eat with him, and he with me."

Then as Jesus was at the table with these two from Emmaus, he took a bit of bread, gave thanks, broke it, and began to give it to them. In that instant they recognized him—the scales of doubt and defeat dropped from their eyes, and they beheld him. Their cataracts gave way to a vision of Christ; their eyes were opened and their spirits caught fire.

In that moment they realized that life had risen above death, and their hearts grew strong. What had been a series of broken threads was now revealed as a grand tapestry of God's grace and faithfulness.

A man was carefully looking at a painting in the Art Institute in Chicago when he was joined by a small boy who stood beside him for a moment. They were both looking at a crucifixion scene from one of the masters of the Renaissance. The man, wondering what the little boy understood about the scene, said, "What is that painting about?"

The boy said, "Don't ya know? That's Jesus and those people around him killed him; they killed him until he was dead."

The man, satisfied that the boy knew, turned and started to walk away. He had only taken a few steps when he heard the voice of the boy calling to him, "Mister! Mister!" The man turned. *"He didn't stay dead, ya know. He didn't stay dead,"* the boy said.

That is the single truth that trumps our fears and doubts. It is the answer to every hurt and disappointment in history. He didn't stay dead!

As these followers of Jesus began to grasp that truth for themselves, the stranger in their midst disappeared. They turned and said to each other, "Were not our hearts burning within us while he talked with us on the road and opened the Scriptures to us?"

Immediately they started back to Jerusalem. Their hearts had become altars and God's spirit the flame as they moved with the setting sun behind them and the promise of an eternal "Son rise" before them. —JB

***After reading the passage from Luke 24 and the
devotional reflection "Sunset, Sunrise," you may also
want to read the following related passages:***
Acts 2:14a, 36-41; Psalm 116:1-4, 12-19; 1 Peter 1:17-23

The **discussion prompts** that follow will help prepare you to participate in your Sunday school class or small-group study. Use your **reflective journaling** section to record any other insights that come to you as you read the Gospel lesson and the devotional reflection.

DISCUSSION PROMPT #1: LUKE 24

Emmaus has been described as "the ordinary places and experiences of our lives, and . . . the places to which we retreat when life is too much for us." With that in mind, where are the Emmaus places in your life?

DISCUSSION PROMPT #2: DEVOTIONAL REFLECTION

The devotional writer suggests that the two disciples on the road to Emmaus begin walking sadly into the sunset but end up running headlong toward the sunrise. Explain what the writer is suggesting with that thought. How does this devotional reflection enrich your understanding of this familiar story?

DISCUSSION PROMPT #3: LUKE 24

Why did the two disciples need Jesus' explanation of Scriptures to understand the importance of what had happened in Jerusalem? Why do we need the same thing?

DISCUSSION PROMPT #4: LUKE 24

"When he was at the table with them" (v. 30) may describe an everyday meal or it could be an observance of Holy Communion. How have you recognized the presence of Jesus in either of those experiences?

REFLECTIVE JOURNALING

_____

_____

_____

_____

_____

_____

_____

_____

_____

_____

ASHES TO FIRE

PSALM 25 ▪ DANIEL 4:19-27 ▪ 1 JOHN 3:19—4:6 ▪ LUKE 4:14-30

MORNING MEDITATIONS

PRAYER—O God, you are the giver of all good gifts and I desire to praise your name for all of your goodness to me. I thank you for sending your Son to die for my sins, for the means of grace, and for the hope of glory, through Jesus Christ. Amen. **JW**

PSALM 25:8-10—Good and upright is the LORD; therefore he instructs sinners in the way. He leads the humble in what is right, and teaches the humble his way. All the paths of the LORD are steadfast love and faithfulness for those who keep his covenant.

DANIEL 4:27 *Righteousness and Mercy*
Therefore, O king, may my counsel be acceptable for you: atone for your sins with righteousness, and your iniquities with mercy to the oppressed, so that your prosperity may be prolonged.

1 JOHN 3:23-24 *That We Should Believe*
And this is his commandment: that we should believe in the name of his Son Jesus Christ and love one another, just as he has commanded us. All who obey his commandments abide in him, and he abides in them. And by this we know that he abides in us, by the Spirit that he has given us.

LUKE 4:14-30 *Today's Gospel Reading*

My friends, if we keep God's commandments in a true loving comradeship together, so that our sins may be forgiven for that love's sake, we are blessed indeed . . . and this blessing was theirs who were chosen by God in Jesus Christ our Lord.

FROM A LETTER OF CLEMENT TO THE CORINTHIAN CHURCHES

EVENING REFLECTIONS

PSALM 15:1-2, 3b—O LORD, who may abide in your tent? Who may dwell on your holy hill? Those who walk blamelessly, and do what is right, and speak the truth from their heart; who . . . do no evil to their friends, nor take up a reproach against their neighbors.

PRAYER—O God, fill my soul with so entire a love for you, that I may love nothing but you. Give me grace to study your knowledge daily, that the more I know you, the more I may love you, through Jesus Christ my Lord. Amen. **JW**

TUESDAY

PSALM 28 ▪ DANIEL 4:28-37 ▪ 1 JOHN 4:7-21 ▪ LUKE 4:31-37

MORNING MEDITATIONS

PRAYER—Lord of all life and power, through the mighty resurrection of Jesus, you have overcome sin and death to make all things new in him. This is the day you have made; I will rejoice and be glad in it. Amen.

PSALM 28:6-7—Blessed be the LORD, for he has heard the sound of my pleadings. The LORD is my strength and my shield; in him my heart trusts; so I am helped, and my heart exults, and with my song I give thanks to him.

DANIEL 4:34 *Everlasting King*
I, Nebuchadnezzar, lifted my eyes . . . I blessed the Most High, and praised and honored the one who lives forever. For his sovereignty is an everlasting sovereignty, and his kingdom endures from generation to generation.

1 JOHN 4:11-12 *We Believe the Love God Has for Us*
Beloved, since God loved us so much, we also ought to love one another. No one has ever seen God; if we love one another, God lives in us, and his love is perfected in us.

LUKE 4:31-37 *Today's Gospel Reading*

Yet there is in the experience of God this insistent, imperative, glorious yearning—the craving for complete spotlessness of the inner self before him.

FROM THOMAS KELLY, *A TESTAMENT OF DEVOTION*

EVENING REFLECTIONS

PSALM 36:7, 9—How precious is your steadfast love, O God! All people may take refuge in the shadow of your wings . . . for with you is the fountain of life; in your light we see light.

PRAYER—O Lamb of God, give me grace throughout my whole life, in every thought, and word and work, to imitate your meekness and humility. May I go through all the scenes of life not seeking my own glory, but looking wholly unto you, and acting wholly for you, through Christ my Lord. Amen. *JW*

PSALM 38 ▪ DANIEL 5:1-12 ▪ 1 JOHN 5:1-12 ▪ LUKE 4:38-44

MORNING MEDITATIONS

PRAYER—Lord God, send your Holy Spirit to be the guide of all my ways and the sanctifier of my soul and body. Give me the light of your presence, your peace from heaven, and the salvation of my soul, through Jesus Christ my Lord. Amen. *JW*

PSALM 38:9-10a, 21-22—O Lord, all my longing is known to you; my sighing is not hidden from you. My heart throbs, my strength fails me . . . Do not forsake me, O LORD; O my God, do not be far from me; make haste to help me, O Lord, my salvation.

DANIEL 5:3-5a   *The Fingers of a Human Hand*
So they brought in the vessels of gold and silver that had been taken out of the temple, the house of God in Jerusalem, and the king and his lords . . . drank from them . . . and praised the gods of gold and silver, bronze, iron, wood, and stone. Immediately, the fingers of a human hand appeared and began writing on the plaster of the wall.

1 JOHN 5:3-4a   *His Commands Are Not a Burden*
For the love of God is this, that we obey his commandments. And his commandments are not burdensome, for whatever is born of God conquers the world.

LUKE 4:38-44   *Today's Gospel Reading*

The life that intends to be wholly obedient, wholly submissive, wholly listening, is astonishing in its completeness. Its joys are ravishing, its peace profound, its humility the deepest, its power world-shaking, its love enveloping, its simplicity that of a trusting child.   A QUOTE FROM THOMAS KELLY, *A TESTAMENT OF DEVOTION*

EVENING REFLECTIONS

PSALM 119:32-34—I run the way of your commandments . . . Teach me, O LORD, the way of your statutes, and I will observe it to the end. Give me understanding, that I may keep your law and observe it with my whole heart.

PRAYER—Father, grant me forgiveness of what is past, that in the days to come I may with a pure spirit do your will—walking humbly with you, showing love to all, and keeping body and soul in sanctification and honor, in Jesus' name. Amen. *JW*

PSALM 37:1-18 ▪ DANIEL 5:13-30 ▪ 1 JOHN 5:13-20 ▪ LUKE 5:1-11

MORNING MEDITATIONS

PRAYER—Eternal God, my Sovereign Lord, I acknowledge all I am, all I have is yours. I humbly thank you for all the blessings you have bestowed upon me—for creating me in your own image, for redeeming me by the death of your blessed Son, and for the assistance of the Holy Spirit, through Christ I pray. Amen. **JW**

PSALM 37:1a, 3-5—Do not fret because of the wicked . . . Trust in the LORD, and do good; so you will live in the land and enjoy security. Take delight in the LORD, and he will give you the desires of your heart. Commit your way to the LORD; trust in him, and he will act.

DANIEL 5:23, 26-28   *You Have Not Honored God*
"You have praised the gods . . . which do not see or hear or know; but the God in whose power is your very breath, and to whom belongs all your ways, you have not honored. . . . This is the interpretation of the [writing]: God has numbered the days of your kingdom . . . you have been weighed on the scales and found wanting . . . your kingdom is divided."

1 JOHN 5:20   *The True God Is Eternal Life*
And we know that the Son of God has come and has given us understanding so that we may know him who is true; and we are in him who is true, in his Son Jesus Christ. He is the true God and eternal life.

LUKE 5:1-11   *Today's Gospel Reading*

The Father of immortality sent his immortal Son, who is the Word, into the world. He came to men to wash them with water and the Spirit. To regenerate us to incorruptibility of mind and body, he breathed into us the spirit of life.

A READING FROM A TREATISE BY HIPPOLYTUS

EVENING REFLECTIONS

PSALM 37:25, 27—I have been young, and now am old, yet I have not seen the righteous forsaken or their children begging bread . . . Depart from evil, and do good.

PRAYER—To you, O God, Father, Son, and Holy Spirit, my Creator, Redeemer, and Sanctifier, I give up myself entirely; may I no longer serve myself, but you only, all the days of my life, through Christ my Lord, I pray. Amen. **JW**

FRIDAY
WEEK 3
EASTER SEASON

PSALM 105:1-22 ▪ DANIEL 6:1-18 ▪ 2 JOHN 1-13 ▪ LUKE 5:12-26

MORNING MEDITATIONS

PRAYER—Almighty God, I bless you from my heart. O Savior of the World, God of God, Light of Light, you have destroyed the power of the devil, you have overcome death, and you sit at the right hand of the Father. Be today my light and peace and make me a new creature, through Christ my Lord. Amen. *JW*

PSALM 105:4-5, 7—Seek the LORD and his strength; seek his presence continually. Remember the wonderful works he has done, his miracles, and the judgments he has uttered . . . He is the LORD our God; his judgments are in all the earth.

DANIEL 6:13, 16 *Daniel Was Thrown into the Den of Lions*
Then they responded to the king, "Daniel, one of the exiles from Judah, pays no attention to you, O king, or to the interdict you have signed, but he is saying his prayers three times a day . . . Then the king gave the command, and Daniel was brought and thrown into the den of lions. The king said, "May your God, whom you faithfully serve, deliver you."

2 JOHN 9 *Abide in the Teaching of Christ*
Everyone who does not abide in the teaching of Christ, but goes beyond it, does not have God; whoever abides in the teaching has both the Father and the Son.

LUKE 5:12-26 *Today's Gospel Reading*

Linked with Jesus? Then linked with life and immortality. He is Life Eternal, unkillable; He is Energy itself, undying, unquenchable. Let him flood your being and lift you above defeat and inertia. So long as he has work for you to do, he can quicken your mortal body here and now.   BERTHA MUNRO

EVENING REFLECTIONS

PSALM 105:42, 43, 45—He remembered his holy promise . . . So he brought his people out with joy, his chosen ones with singing . . . that they might keep his statutes and observe his laws. Praise the LORD!

PRAYER—Father, accept my imperfect repentance, show compassion for my infirmities, forgive my faults, purify my motives, strengthen my weakness, and let your good Spirit watch over me, and your love ever rule my heart, through the mercies of Jesus, I pray. Amen. *JW*

136   ASHES TO FIRE

PSALM 30 ▪ DANIEL 6:19-28 ▪ 3 JOHN 1-15 ▪ LUKE 5:27-39

MORNING MEDITATIONS

PRAYER—Lord God, you have left us your holy Word to be a lantern to our feet and a light unto our steps. Give us your Holy Spirit that out of the same Word we may learn what your eternal will is and frame our lives in holy obedience to it, to your honor and glory and increase of our faith, through Jesus Christ our Lord. Amen.

PSALM 30:4-5—Sing praises to the Lord, O you his faithful ones, and give thanks to his holy name. His anger is but for a moment; his favor is for a lifetime. Weeping may linger for the night, but joy comes with the morning.

DANIEL 6:21-23a, 25-26a   *My God Sent His Angel*
Daniel then said to the king, "O king, live forever! My God sent his angel and shut the lions' mouths so that they would not hurt me, because I was found blameless before him" . . . Then the king was exceedingly glad and . . . wrote: "I make a decree, that in all my royal dominion people should tremble and fear before the God of Daniel: for he is the living God.

3 JOHN 11   *Imitate the Good*
Beloved, do not imitate what is evil but imitate what is good. Whoever does good is from God; whoever does evil has not seen God.

LUKE 5:27-39   *Today's Gospel Reading*

We must therefore, make an offering to God and show ourselves in everything grateful to him who made us, in the purity of our thoughts, the sincerity of our faith, the firmness of our hope and our burning charity.   A READING FROM A TREATISE BY IRENAEUS

EVENING REFLECTIONS

PSALM 42:1-2a, 8—As a deer longs for flowing streams, so my soul longs for you, O God. My soul thirsts for God, for the living God . . . By day the Lord commands his steadfast love; and at night his song is with me, a prayer to the God of my life.

PRAYER—Now to God the Father who first loved us and made us accepted in the Beloved; to God the Son who loved us and washed us from our sins in his own blood; to God the Holy Spirit who sheds the love of God abroad in our hearts, be all love and all glory for time and for eternity. Amen. **JW**

WEEK FOUR

EASTER SEASON

Ashes to Fire Week 10

Sunday: With Jesus at a Sheepfold

Read the Gospel passage from John 10:1-11, the devotional reflection titled "The Good Life," and respond to the discussion prompts in the Reflective Journaling section.

THE MUSIC OF ASHES TO FIRE

Week 10: "Our Desire" (Track 11)

Monday through Saturday of Easter Season Week 4

IN THE MORNING:

A personal daily devotional guide includes prayer, a reading from the Old Testament, the Psalms, the Epistles, and the Gospel for each day of the week.

This week's readings are from Genesis, Exodus, Colossians, and the Gospel of Luke.

Inspirational quotes from men and women of faith keep us in contact with our shared Christian heritage.

IN THE EVENING:

An evening psalm and prayer become preludes to nighttime rest and renewal.

EASTER SEASON–WEEK FOUR
With Jesus at a Sheepfold

A devotional reflection based on John 10:1-11

Read the Gospel passage first, then the devotional reflection that follows. The discussion prompts at the end will help prepare you for Sunday school and small-group sessions.

The Good Life

There is perhaps no image that evokes such an array of truth about God and the relationship we can have with him as the picture of Jesus as the Good Shepherd. This idea is interwoven throughout the Scriptures and is particularly used by John in his Gospel to help us understand the connection God offers us through Christ.

In John 10, Jesus' habit of conveying truth poetically rather than propositionally is clearly on display. Jesus speaks of sheepfolds, gates, thieves, sheep, gatekeepers, strangers, and voices. In these word pictures several key ideas are introduced: intimacy, protection, guidance, care, and access to the fullness of life are all linked directly to Jesus.

- *Intimacy:* "He calls his own sheep by name. . . . his sheep follow him because they know his voice" (v. 3).
- *Protection:* The "shepherd lays down his life for the sheep"(v. 11). Jesus stands as the gate to guard the sheep from danger.
- *Guidance:* Notice that the shepherd leads rather than drives his sheep. The sheep are led by the voice of the master: "His sheep follow him because they know his voice" (v. 4). This suggests intimacy and relationship. To hear his voice means both to listen *and* give heed. What good is hearing Jesus if we don't heed him? Jesus can lead only if we follow.

- **Care:** The shepherd's primary role is to see that the sheep have all they need. "I came that they may have life, and have it abundantly" (v. 10).
- **Access:** Through Jesus and him alone we find access to God. The sheep "will come in and go out and find pasture" (v. 9).

All of these ideas are wrapped up in the two key phrases in this passage: "I tell you the truth, I am the gate for the sheep," and "I have come that they may have life and have it to the full." Charlotte Denny notes, "For half the world's population the brutal reality is this: you'd be better off as a cow. The average European cow receives $2.20 (£1.40) a day from the taxpayer in subsidies and other aid. Meanwhile, 2.8 billion people in developing countries around the world live on less than $2 a day."* In such a world, what does it mean to have the fullness of life?

In this passage, life is more than the opposite of death. It is that, but there is more, much more. The abundant life of John 10 is a complex image. It links the sheep pen and the pasture by way of "the gate." It is through the gate that the sheep may safely go in and out. Life inside and outside the pen are linked by the One who is "the way."

The existence of thieves, wolves, and other dangers is described in very real terms, and yet this does not mean that the sheep are to be shut in and overprotected, for their food is out beyond the pen. There is a gate and a shepherd—the Lord Jesus, himself.

The imagery of Jesus as the gate suggests a doorkeeper as well as guardian. He decides who does or does not enter the fold. Our Lord himself desires to be the guardian of our lives. However, we must be determined to hear him, heed him, and stay close by him. Through the Holy Spirit, he will help us to recognize his voice from the false voices of our world.

The "I am the gate/door" statement in John 10:7 is one of the seven "I am" sayings of Jesus in the Gospel of John.
- "I am the bread of life."
- "I am the light of the world."
- "I am the gate/door."
- "I am the good shepherd."
- "I am the resurrection and the life."

---

*Charlotte Denny, "Cows are better off than half the world," *The Guardian,* August 22, 2002.

- "I am the way, the truth and the life."
- "I am the vine."

Every time Jesus makes an "I am" statement, he uses the Greek terms *eimi* and *ho*. *Ego eimi* are emphatic words that mean "I was, am, and will be." *Ho* means "the," not "a." The idea being that Jesus is not *a* door. He is not one of *many* doors. Jesus says that he is *the* door or gate.

The abundant life Jesus promises is a life filled with meaning and purpose. "Abundant" means "superior in quality, exceeding and beyond measure." This is the life promised by Jesus. However, it is not a consumer promise; it is a way-of-living promise. It is abundance no matter what one's circumstances. The word "life" really translates into a "way to live." Jesus has come to bring us a *way to live abundantly*. That is not just a future promise but a today promise as well.

A primary characteristic of a good shepherd is that he is willing to die for the sheep. Thus this passage is foreshadowing that Jesus was willing to die on the cross that others might live. John uses this phrase, *"lays his life down,"* in John 13:37; 15:13; and 1 John 3:16. In this passage here in John 10, the phrase *"lays his life down"* is used five times within one chapter.

Notice also that Christ is not only the gate *into* the sheepfold but also the gate *out* to green pastures. One side of the metaphor is this: Christ is the gate *into* the sheepfold where we will find protection from the wolves of life. The other side of the metaphor is that Jesus is the gate by which we go *out* to green pastures and experience the fullness of life and the abundant life. —JB

After reading the passage from John 10 and the devotional reflection "The Good Life" you may also want to read the following related passages:
Acts 2:42-47; Psalm 23; 1 Peter 2:19-25

The **discussion prompts** that follow will help prepare you to participate in your Sunday school class or small-group study. Use your **reflective journaling** section to record any other insights that come to you as you read the Gospel lesson and the devotional reflection.

DISCUSSION PROMPT #1: JOHN 10
Even though the people who were listening to Jesus on that day were familiar with sheep and shepherds, "they did not understand what he was saying to

them" (v. 6). What is another "figure of speech" (v. 6) that could be used today to make the same point Jesus was making?

DISCUSSION PROMPT #2: JOHN

Sheep and shepherds have been a dominant metaphor for the relationships of the church with Jesus and within the community of faith we know as the church. What else can you say about how these images describe Jesus and us beyond what is said in this particular passage?

DISCUSSION PROMPT #3: JOHN 10

"The sheep follow [the shepherd] because they know his voice" (v. 4). How do you distinguish Jesus' voice from all the different voices competing for your attention in today's world?

DISCUSSION PROMPT #4: DEVOTIONAL REFLECTION

The devotional writer notes that the word *life* translates into *a way to live*. In what ways does Jesus provide you with a way to live abundantly?

REFLECTIVE JOURNALING

_____

_____

_____

_____

_____

_____

_____

_____

_____

_____

_____

PSALM 41 ▪ GENESIS 32:1-20 ▪ COLOSSIANS 1:1-14 ▪ LUKE 6:1-11

MORNING MEDITATIONS

PRAYER—O God, you are the giver of all good gifts and I desire to praise your name for all of your goodness to me. I thank you for sending your Son to die for my sins, for the means of grace, and for the hope of glory, through Jesus Christ. Amen. **JW**

PSALM 41:4, 12—As for me, I said, "O LORD, be gracious to me; heal me, for I have sinned against you" . . . But you have upheld me because of my integrity, and set me in your presence forever."

GENESIS 32:9a, 10a, 12   *Not Worthy*
And Jacob said, "O God of my father Abraham and God of my father Isaac . . . I am not worthy of the least of all thy steadfast love and all the faithfulness that you have shown to your servant . . . Yet you have said, 'I will surely do you good, and make your offspring as the sand of the sea.'"

COLOSSIANS 1:11b-12   *Joyfully Giving Thanks*
May you be prepared to endure everything with patience, while joyfully giving thanks to the Father, who has enabled you to share in the inheritance of the saints in the light.

LUKE 6:1-11   *Today's Gospel Reading*

But what is perfection? The word has various sense: it means perfect love. It is love excluding sin; love filling the heart, taking up the whole capacity of the soul. It is love "rejoicing evermore, praying without ceasing, in everything giving thanks."
AN EXCERPT FROM JOHN WESLEY'S SERMON *THE SCRIPTURE WAY OF SALVATION*

EVENING REFLECTIONS

PSALM 44:1, 26—We have heard with our ears, O God; our ancestors have told us, what deed you performed in their days, in the days of old . . . Come to our help, redeem us for the sake of your steadfast love.

PRAYER—O God, fill my soul with so entire a love for you, that I may love nothing but you. Give me grace to study your knowledge daily, that the more I know you, the more I may love you, through Jesus Christ my Lord. Amen. **JW**

PSALM 45 ▪ GENESIS 32:21-34 ▪ COLOSSIANS 1:15-23 ▪ LUKE 6:12-26

MORNING MEDITATIONS

PRAYER—Lord of all life and power, through the mighty resurrection of Jesus, you have overcome sin and death to make all things new in him. This is the day you have made; I will rejoice and be glad in it. Amen.

PSALM 45:6-7a—Your throne, O God, endures forever and ever. Your royal scepter is scepter of equity; you love righteousness and hate wickedness.

GENESIS 32:24, 26-28   *The Night Wrestler*
Jacob was left alone and a man wrestled with him until daybreak . . . Then he said, "Let me go, for the day is breaking." But Jacob said, "I will not let you go, unless you bless me." So the man said, "What is your name?" And he said. "Jacob." Then the man said, "You shall no longer be Jacob, but Israel, for you have striven with God . . . and have prevailed."

COLOSSIANS 1:21-22   *We Are Reconciled*
And you who were once estranged and hostile in mind, doing evil deeds, he has now reconciled in his fleshly body through death, so as to present you holy and blameless and irreproachable before him.

LUKE 6:12-26   *Today's Gospel Reading*

One must come as a mere sinner, inwardly and outwardly, self-destroyed and self-condemned, bringing nothing to God but ungodliness only . . . Thus it is, and thus alone, when his mouth is stopped, and he stands utterly guilty before God, that he can look unto Jesus as the whole and sole sacrifice for his sins.

AN EXCERPT FROM JOHN WESLEY'S SERMON *JUSTIFICATION BY FAITH*

EVENING REFLECTIONS

PSALM 47:1-2, 4—Clap your hands, all you peoples; shout to God with loud songs of joy. For the Lord, the Most High, is awesome, a great king over all the earth . . . He chose our heritage for us, the pride of Jacob whom he loves.

PRAYER—O Lamb of God, give me grace throughout my whole life, in every thought, and word and work, to imitate your meekness and humility. May I go through all the scenes of life not seeking my own glory, but looking wholly unto you, and acting wholly for you, through Christ my Lord. Amen. **JW**

PSALM 119:49-72 ▪ EXODUS 33:1-23 ▪ COLOSSIANS 1:24—2:7 ▪ LUKE 6:27-38

MORNING MEDITATIONS

PRAYER—Lord God, send your Holy Spirit to be the guide of all my ways and the sanctifier of my soul and body. Give me the light of your presence, your peace from heaven, and the salvation of my soul, through Jesus Christ my Lord. Amen. *JW*

PSALM 119:49-50—Remember your word to your servant, in which you have made me hope. This is my comfort in my distress, that your promise gives me life.

EXODUS 33:18-19   *I Will Be Gracious*
Moses said, "Show me your glory, I pray." And he said, "I will make all my goodness pass before you, and will proclaim before you the name, 'The LORD'; and I will be gracious to whom I will be gracious, and will show mercy on whom I will show mercy."

COLOSSIANS 2:6-7   *Continue to Live in Christ*
As you have received Christ Jesus the Lord, continue to live your lives in him, rooted and built up in him and established in the faith, just as you were taught, abounding in thanksgiving.

LUKE 6:27-38   *Today's Gospel Reading*

All who expect to be sanctified at all expect to be sanctified by faith. But in the meantime, they know that faith will not be given but to them that obey.

AN EXCERPT FROM A LETTER OF JOHN WESLEY TO MS. FURLEY

EVENING REFLECTIONS

PSALM 119:55-56—I remember your name in the night, O LORD, and keep your law. This blessing has fallen to me, for I have kept your precepts.

PRAYER—Father, grant me forgiveness of what is past, that in the days to come I may with a pure spirit do your will—walking humbly with you, showing love to all, and keeping body and soul in sanctification and honor, in Jesus' name. Amen. *JW*

THURSDAY

WEEK 4
EASTER SEASON

PSALM 50 ▪ EXODUS 34:1-17 ▪ COLOSSIANS 2:8-23 ▪ LUKE 6:39-49

MORNING MEDITATIONS

PRAYER—Eternal God, my Sovereign Lord, I acknowledge all I am, all I have is yours. I humbly thank you for all the blessings you have bestowed upon me—for creating me in your own image, for redeeming me by the death of your blessed Son, and for the assistance of the Holy Spirit, through Christ I pray. Amen. **JW**

PSALM 50:1-2—The mighty one, God the Lord, speaks and summons the earth from the rising of the sun to its setting. Out of Zion, the perfection of beauty, God shines forth.

EXODUS 34:6-7b   *Pardon Our Iniquity*
The Lord passed before him, and proclaimed, "The Lord, the Lord, a God merciful and gracious, slow to anger, and abounding in steadfast love and faithfulness . . . forgiving iniquity and transgression and sin."

COLOSSIANS 2:12-14a   *Raised with Christ Through Faith*
When you were buried with [Christ] in baptism, you were also raised with him through faith in the power of God . . . And when you were dead in trespasses . . . God made you alive with him when he forgave us all our trespasses, erasing the record that stood against us with its legal demands.

LUKE 6:39-49   *Today's Gospel Reading*

You are a child of God, a member of Christ, an heir of the kingdom. What you have, hold fast, and you shall have all that God has prepared for them that love him . . . You cannot live on what he did yesterday. Therefore he comes today . . . to destroy anything . . . that is not of God.   AN EXCERPT FROM A LETTER OF JOHN WESLEY

EVENING REFLECTIONS

PSALM 59:16b-17—You have been a fortress for me and a refuge in the day of my distress. O my strength, I will sing praises to you, for you, O God, are my fortress, the God who shows me steadfast love.

PRAYER—O my God, I love you above all things, with my whole heart and soul, because you are worthy of all my love. I forgive all who have injured me, and I ask pardon for all whom I may have injured. Amen.

PSALM 40 ▪ EXODUS 34:18-35 ▪ COLOSSIANS 3:1-11 ▪ LUKE 7:1-17

MORNING MEDITATIONS

PRAYER—Almighty God, I bless you from my heart. O Savior of the World, God of God, Light of Light, you have destroyed the power of the devil, you have overcome death, and you sit at the right hand of the Father. Be today my light and peace and make me a new creature, through Christ my Lord. Amen. *JW*

PSALM 40:5—You have multiplied, O Lord my God, your wondrous deeds and your thoughts toward us; none can compare with you. Were I to proclaim and tell of them, they would be more than can be counted.

EXODUS 34:29 *His Face Shone*
Moses came down from Mount Sinai. As he came down from the mountain with the two tablets of the covenant in his hand, Moses did not know that the skin of his face shone because he had been talking with God.

COLOSSIANS 3:2-4 *Set Your Minds on Things Above*
Set your minds on things that are above, not on things that are on earth, for you have died, and your life is hidden with Christ in God. When Christ who is your life is revealed, then you also will be revealed with him in glory.

LUKE 7:1-17 *Today's Gospel Reading*

The God of love is willing to save all the souls that he has made. This he has proclaimed to them in his Word, together with the terms of salvation, revealed by the Son of his love, who gave his own life that they who believe in him might have everlasting life.

AN EXCERPT FROM JOHN WESLEY'S SERMON, *THE WEDDING GARMENT*

EVENING REFLECTIONS

PSALM 51:6, 9—You desire truth in the inward being, therefore teach me wisdom in my secret heart. . . . Hide your face from my sins, and blot out all my iniquities.

PRAYER—Father, accept my imperfect repentance, show compassion for my infirmities, forgive my faults, purify my motives, strengthen my weakness, and let your good Spirit watch over me, and your love ever rule my heart, through the mercies of Jesus, I pray. Amen. *JW*

PSALM 55 ▪ EXODUS 40:18-38 ▪ COLOSSIANS 3:12-4:18 ▪ LUKE 7:18-28, 31-35

MORNING MEDITATIONS

PRAYER—Lord of all life and power, through the mighty resurrection of Jesus, you have overcome sin and death to make all things new in him. This is the day you have made; I will rejoice and be glad in it. Amen.

PSALM 55:16-18a—But I call upon God, and the LORD will save me. Evening and morning and at noon I utter my complaint and moan, and he will hear my voice. He will redeem me unharmed from the battle that I wage.

EXODUS 40:18a, 33-34 *Moses Finished the Work*
Moses set up the tabernacle . . . He set up the court around the tabernacle and the altar, and put up the screen at the gate of the court. So Moses finished the work. Then the cloud covered the tent of meeting, and the glory of the LORD filled the tabernacle.

COLOSSIANS 3:12, 14 *Clothe Yourselves with Love*
As God's chosen ones, holy and beloved, clothe yourselves with compassion, kindness, humility, meekness, and patience . . . Above all, clothe yourselves with love, which binds everything together in perfect harmony.

LUKE 7:18-28, 31-35 *Today's Gospel Reading*

You judge rightly. Perfect love and Christian liberty are the very same things . . . and what is Christian liberty but another word for holiness . . . Holiness is the love of God and man, or the mind which was in Christ.

AN EXCERPT FROM A LETTER BY JOHN WESLEY TO JOSEPH BENSON

EVENING REFLECTIONS

PSALM 139:11-12, 23—If I say, "Surely the darkness shall cover me, and the light around me become night," even the darkness is not dark to you; the night is as bright as the day, for darkness is as light to you . . . Search me, O God, and know my heart; test me and know my thoughts.

PRAYER—Now to God the Father who first loved us and made us accepted in the Beloved; to God the Son who loved us and washed us from our sins in his own blood; to God the Holy Spirit who sheds the love of God abroad in our hearts, be all love and all glory for time and for eternity. Amen. *JW*

WEEK FIVE
EASTER SEASON

Ashes to Fire Week 11

Sunday: With Jesus and the Disciples (1)

Read the Gospel passage from John 14:1-14, the devotional reflection titled "Which Way Should I Turn?" and respond to the discussion prompts in the Reflective Journaling section.

THE MUSIC OF ASHES TO FIRE

Week 11: "When Amidst the Storm I'm Shaken" (Track 12)

Monday through Saturday of Easter Season Week 5

IN THE MORNING:

A personal daily devotional guide includes prayer, a reading from the Old Testament, the Psalms, the Epistles, and the Gospel for each day of the week.

This week's readings are from Isaiah, Romans, Colossians, and the Gospel of Luke.

Inspirational quotes from men and women of faith keep us in contact with our shared Christian heritage.

IN THE EVENING:

An evening psalm and prayer become preludes to nighttime rest and renewal.

EASTER SEASON—WEEK FIVE
With Jesus and the Disciples (1)

A devotional reflection based on John 14:1-14

Read the Gospel passage first, then the devotional reflection that follows. The discussion prompts at the end will help prepare you for Sunday school and small-group sessions.

Which Way Should I Turn?

All day long a dreary dampness seeped through my light jacket, and now darkness descended as I searched for any place to park the VW Rabbit. A space to park is a rare find on the cramped streets deep inside the city. The drizzle quickened and the night grew darker as I turned onto the narrow avenue leading to the county hospital. I had been here months before on a bright sunny day, but my friend drove that day because he knew his way. This night, however, I was alone, without a map, cell phone, or GPS, and nothing was familiar.

I checked the street sign again to make sure I was going the right way. Through the gloomy rain it was difficult to read, but yes, it was Cornel Street. So why did none of the deeply shadowed buildings remind me of my earlier visit? I shivered and pushed the heat symbol on the dash as I strained to see beyond the swishing wipers, hoping to find any available spot or recognizable structure. Then a flash lit the sky and I heard the crashing boom of thunder. Suddenly, the streetlights blanked out and everything was dark except for a blinking red light blocks away.

If I drove around the block, I reasoned, maybe a parking space would open. At the corner I took a right only to find road construction forcing me to detour to the next block before I could turn. Again there was no place to park. I made a right turn at the next corner. Once more every space was filled. At the end of that block I paused at a flashing red light and turned right again, expecting that at the next corner my trip around the block would be completed back to Cornel Street. But instead, I found myself driving down a long narrow one-way street without any side roads. Lightning flashed, and in the distance another blinking light offered hope of finding my way through the darkened streets and unreadable signs.

At the flickering red light, I turned right and continued to a stop sign straight ahead. The intersection there hosted three converging unlit streets lined with parked and locked cars.

I had no clue about the names of the streets, where they led, or which one I was on. I had to admit I was lost, lost in a strange city on a cold, starless night. I felt as if the freezing rain had suddenly dropped a curtain of isolation and dread all around me. I was alone and didn't know which way to turn.

Have you ever felt the frustrating bewilderment of not knowing which way to turn? Stress and anxiety easily slip in when we don't know where to go. Sometimes we know exactly where we are but still feel lost and perplexed. Turbulent circumstances can disorient us and rob our quiet confidence for life. Precisely at that point Jesus has something to say to us if we will listen.

In John 14, the disciples wanted to see and know God. Their last few years with Jesus had been exhilarating, but nagging doubts fed perplexing questions. They wanted simple answers clearly showing the way. They wanted God to set everything straight, make things right, and establish his mighty kingdom.

They had their King. Jesus was their man. Miraculous power and supernatural interventions had them convinced, but his teachings on how to find life through death overwhelmed their logic. The disciples thought victory and triumph, while Jesus spoke of betrayal and death. They anticipated ease and comfort, but Jesus taught self-denial and the cross. They lived in tension and fear, but Jesus radiated calm and peace.

Bewildered, they pleaded, "Just show us the way; show us the Father and it will be enough." All the while, they wondered, *How can the way to life and power be through suffering and death?* Jesus tried to prepare them for the time when their world would be completely upset, turned on its head and collapsed in utter chaos and confusion.

What can we do when our expectations get turned upside down? When circumstances move beyond our control and we are forced to admit we don't know which way to turn, what can we do then?

In those moments we must turn to Jesus and hear him say, "Let not your hearts be troubled. You trust God, Trust me. I am telling you the truth. I am preparing a place for you so that you might be with me forever. Where I am is heaven and where I AM is your destiny, your eternal home" (John 14:1-3, author's paraphrase).

We can trust Jesus. Many people tell us the truth, but only Jesus says, "I AM the truth." When frightening anxieties fill our lives, Truth invites us to trust him. When we don't know which way to turn, Truth says, "I AM the way; trust me."

Imagine going to an unfamiliar city and asking for directions. The person says, "Take the first turn to the right, and the second to the left. Cross the square and go past the church and take the third turn on the right, and the road you want is the fourth road on the left. You can't miss it."

We would be lost before we got to the second turn. But if the person says, "Come. Follow me. I know the way; I'll take you there," that person for us becomes the way.

Jesus desires to take us by the hand and lead us down life's uncertain paths to the place he has prepared for us. His Word provides guidance and counsel for every stage of the journey. We can trust Jesus every step of the way. With wide open arms, he invites us, "Turn to me. Trust me. Follow me. I AM your true way to real life now and forever." —WS

After reading the passage from John 14 and the devotional reflection "Trust and Obey" you may also want to read the following related passages:
Acts 7:55-60; Psalm 31:1-5, 15-16; 1 Peter 2:2-10

The **discussion prompts** that follow will help prepare you to participate in your Sunday school class or small-group study. Use your **reflective journaling** section to record any other insights that come to you as you read the Gospel lesson and the devotional reflection.

DISCUSSION PROMPT #1: JOHN 14
This passage is among the most well-known of all the Scriptures. What are these verses describing?

DISCUSSION PROMPT #2: JOHN 14
Is this description limited to only the after-life? Why or why not?

DISCUSSION PROMPT #3: JOHN 14

How do we "know the way to the place where [Jesus] is going" (v. 4b)? Name some of the various ways in which God allows us to know the way.

DISCUSSION PROMPT #4: JOHN 14

What could be some ways of understanding "in my Father's house there are many dwelling places" (v. 2a)?

DISCUSSION PROMPT #5: DEVOTIONAL REFLECTION

How does the personal experience of the devotional writer in "Which Way Should I Turn?" help you with your own understanding of this passage?

REFLECTIVE JOURNALING

_____

_____

_____

_____

_____

_____

_____

_____

_____

_____

_____

_____

_____

_____

_____

_____

_____

_____

PSALM 56 ▪ ISAIAH 60:1-16 ▪ COLOSSIANS 3:18—4:18 ▪ LUKE 7:36-50

MORNING MEDITATIONS

PRAYER—O God, you are the giver of all good gifts and I desire to praise your name for all of your goodness to me. I thank you for sending your Son to die for my sins, for the means of grace, and for the hope of glory, through Jesus Christ. Amen. **JW**

PSALM 56:12-13—My vows to you I must perform, O God; I will render thank offerings to you. For you have delivered my soul from death, and my feet from falling, so that I may walk before God in the light of life.

ISAIAH 60:1, 15b, 16c   *Majestic Forever*
Arise, shine; for your light has come, and the glory of the Lord has risen upon you . . . I will make you majestic forever, a joy from age to age . . . you shall know that I, the Lord, am your Savior and your Redeemer, the Mighty One of Jacob.

COLOSSIANS 3:4-5   *Conduct Yourselves Wisely*
Conduct yourselves wisely toward outsiders, making the most of the time. Let your speech always be gracious, seasoned with salt, so that you may know how you ought to answer everyone.

LUKE 7:36-50   *Today's Gospel Reading*

> For Christ's resurrection is life for the dead, pardon for sinners, glory for the saints . . .
> The light of Christ is day without night, day without end. When Christ's light draws near, the darkness of the devil is put to flight, and the shadows of sin do not approach.
>
> A QUOTE FROM THE SERMONS OF MAXIMUS OF TURIN

EVENING REFLECTIONS

PSALM 65:3, 5—When deeds of iniquity overwhelm us, you forgive our transgressions . . . By awesome deeds you answer us with deliverance, O God of our salvation; you are the hope of all the ends of the earth and of the farthest seas.

PRAYER—O God, fill my soul with so entire a love for you, that I may love nothing but you. Give me grace to study your knowledge daily, that the more I know you, the more I may love you, through Jesus Christ my Lord. Amen. **JW**

PSALM 61 ▪ ISAIAH 60:17-22 ▪ ROMANS 12:1-21 ▪ LUKE 8:1-15

MORNING MEDITATIONS

PRAYER—Lord of all life and power, through the mighty resurrection of Jesus, you have overcome sin and death to make all things new in him. This is the day you have made; I will rejoice and be glad in it. Amen.

PSALM 61:1-3—Hear my cry, O God; listen to my prayer. From the end of the earth I call to you, when my heart is faint. Lead me to that rock that is higher than I; for you are my refuge, a strong tower against the enemy.

ISAIAH 60:19 *God Will Be Your Glory*
The sun shall no longer be your light by day, nor for brightness shall the moon give light to you by night; but the LORD will be your everlasting light, and your God will be your glory.

ROMANS 12:2 *Be Transformed*
Do not be conformed to this world, but be transformed by the renewing of your minds, so that you may discern what is the will of God—what is good and acceptable and perfect.

LUKE 8:1-15 *Today's Gospel Reading*

If we want to know what the Mind of the Creator is, we must look at Christ. In Him, we shall discover a Mind that loved His creation so completely that he became a part of it, suffered with and for it, and made it a sharer in His own glory.

AN EXCERPT FROM *CREED OR CHAOS* BY DOROTHY SAYERS

EVENING REFLECTIONS

PSALM 68:7a, 8a, 28—O God, when you went out before your people . . . the earth quaked, the heavens poured down rain at the presence of God . . . Summon your might, O God, show your strength, O God, as you have done for us before.

PRAYER—O Lamb of God, give me grace throughout my whole life, in every thought, and word and work, to imitate your meekness and humility. May I go through all the scenes of life not seeking my own glory, but looking wholly unto you, and acting wholly for you, through Christ my Lord. Amen. **JW**

PSALM 70 ▪ ISAIAH 65:1-16 ▪ ROMANS 13:1-14 ▪ LUKE 8:16-25

MORNING MEDITATIONS

PRAYER—Lord God, send your Holy Spirit to be the guide of all my ways and the sanctifier of my soul and body. Give me the light of your presence, your peace from heaven, and the salvation of my soul, through Jesus Christ my Lord. Amen. **JW**

PSALM 70:4-5—Let all who seek you rejoice and be glad in you. Let those who love your salvation say evermore, "God is great!" But I am poor and needy; hasten to me, O God! You are my help and my deliverer; O Lord, do not delay!

ISAIAH 65:1-2a *You Did Not Call on My Name*
I was ready to be sought out by those who did not ask, to be found by those who did not seek me. I said, "Here I am" . . . to a nation that did not call on my name. I held out my hands all day long to a rebellious people.

ROMANS 13:12b, 13b, 14 *Lay Aside the Works of Darkness*
Let us lay aside the works of darkness and put on the armor of light; let us live honorably as in the day . . . not in quarreling and jealousy. Instead, put on the Lord Jesus Christ, and make no provision for the flesh.

LUKE 8:16-25 *Today's Gospel Reading*

The disciples had seen the strong hands of God twist the crown of thorns into a crown of glory, and in hands as strong as that they knew themselves safe.

AN EXCERPT FROM *CREED OR CHAOS* BY DOROTHY SAYERS

EVENING REFLECTIONS

PSALM 119:73, 75—Your hands have made and fashioned me; give me understanding that I may learn your commandments . . . I know, O Lord, that your judgments are right, and that in faithfulness you have humbled me.

PRAYER—Father, grant me forgiveness of what is past, that in the days to come I may with a pure spirit do your will—walking humbly with you, showing love to all, and keeping body and soul in sanctification and honor, in Jesus' name. Amen. **JW**

PSALM 71 • ISAIAH 65:17-25 • ROMANS 14:1-12 • LUKE 8:26-39

MORNING MEDITATIONS

PRAYER—Eternal God, my Sovereign Lord, I acknowledge all I am, all I have is yours. I humbly thank you for all the blessings you have bestowed upon me—for creating me in your own image, for redeeming me by the death of your blessed Son, and for the assistance of the Holy Spirit, through Christ I pray. Amen. **JW**

PSALM 71:17-18—O God, from my youth you have taught me, and I still proclaim your wondrous deeds. So even to old age and gray hairs, O God, do not forsake me, until I proclaim your might to all the generations to come.

ISAIAH 65:17-18a   *Be Glad in What I Am Creating*
For I am about to create new heavens and a new earth; the former things shall not be remembered or come to mind. Be glad and rejoice forever in what I am creating.

ROMANS 14:10c-12   *Lord of Both the Dead and the Living*
We will all stand before the judgment seat of God. For it is written, "As I live, says the Lord, every knee shall bow to me and every tongue shall give praise to God." So then, each of us will be accountable to God.

LUKE 8:26-39   *Today's Gospel Reading*

Faith in a prayer-hearing God will make a prayer-loving Christian.   ANDREW MURRAY

EVENING REFLECTIONS

PSALM 139:11-12, 23—If I say, "Surely the darkness shall cover me, and the light around me become night," even the darkness is not dark to you; the night is as bright as the day, for darkness is as light to you . . . Search me, O God, and know my heart; test me and know my thoughts.

PRAYER—To you, O God, Father, Son, and Holy Spirit, my Creator, Redeemer, and Sanctifier, I give up myself entirely; may I no longer serve myself, but you only, all the days of my life, through Christ my Lord, I pray. Amen. **JW**

PSALM 106:1-18 ▪ ISAIAH 66:1-13 ▪ ROMANS 14:13-23 ▪ LUKE 8:40-56

MORNING MEDITATIONS

PRAYER—Almighty God, I bless you from my heart. O Savior of the World, God of God, Light of Light, you have destroyed the power of the devil, you have overcome death, and you sit at the right hand of the Father. Be today my light and peace and make me a new creature, through Christ my Lord. Amen. *JW*

PSALM 106:1-3—Praise the Lord! O give thanks to the Lord, for he is good; for his steadfast love endures forever. Who can utter the mighty doings of the Lord, or declare his praise? Happy are those who observe justice, who do righteousness at all times.

ISAIAH 66:1a, 2 *Heaven Is My Throne*
Thus says the Lord: Heaven is my throne and the earth is my footstool . . . All these things my hand has made, and so all these things are mine. But . . . I will look to the humble . . . who trembles at my word.

ROMANS 14:17, 19 *Pursue What Makes for Peace*
For the kingdom of God is not food and drink but righteousness and peace and joy in the Holy Spirit . . . Let us then pursue what makes for peace and for mutual upbuilding.

LUKE 8:40-56 *Today's Gospel Reading*

The disciples had misunderstood practically everything Christ had ever said to them, but no matter; the thing made sense at last, and the meaning was far beyond anything they had dreamed. They had expected a walkover, and they beheld a victory; they had expected an earthly Messiah, and they beheld the Soul of Eternity.

AN EXCERPT FROM *CREED OR CHAOS* BY DOROTHY SAYERS

EVENING REFLECTIONS

PSALM 106:47-48—Save us, O Lord our God, and gather us from among the nations, that we may give thanks to your holy name and glory in your praise. Blessed be the Lord, the God of Israel, from everlasting to everlasting. Let all the people say, "Amen."

PRAYER—Father, accept my imperfect repentance, show compassion for my infirmities, forgive my faults, purify my motives, strengthen my weakness, and let your good Spirit watch over me, and your love ever rule my heart, through the mercies of Jesus, I pray. Amen. *JW*

PSALM 75 ▪ ISAIAH 66:14-24 ▪ ROMANS 15:1-21 ▪ LUKE 9:1-17

MORNING MEDITATIONS

PRAYER—Lord of all life and power, through the mighty resurrection of Jesus, you have overcome sin and death to make all things new in him. This is the day you have made; I will rejoice and be glad in it. Amen.

PSALM 75:1, 7—We give thanks to you, O God; we give thanks; your name is near. People tell of your wondrous deeds . . . it is God who executes judgment, putting down one and lifting up another.

ISAIAH 66:22, 23b   *All Flesh Shall Worship*
For as the new heavens and the new earth, which I will make, shall remain before me, says the LORD; so shall your descendants and your name remain . . . All flesh shall come to worship before me, says the LORD.

ROMANS 15:8-9a   *The Gentiles Shall Glorify God*
Christ has become a servant . . . on behalf of the truth of God in order that he might confirm the promises given to the patriarchs, and in order that the Gentiles might glorify God for his mercy.

LUKE 9:1-17   *Today's Gospel Reading*

The resurrection means that the worst has been met and has been conquered. This puts an ultimate optimism at the heart of things. The resurrection says that no matter how life may seem to go to pieces around you, nevertheless, the last word is love.   E. STANLEY JONES

EVENING REFLECTIONS

PSALM 27:5, 7-8—For he will hide me in his shelter in the day of trouble; he will conceal me under the cover of his tent; he will set me high on a rock . . . Hear, O LORD, when I cry aloud, be gracious to me and answer me! "Come," my heart says, "seek his face!" Your face, LORD, do I seek.

PRAYER—Now to God the Father who first loved us and made us accepted in the Beloved; to God the Son who loved us and washed us from our sins in his own blood; to God the Holy Spirit who sheds the love of God abroad in our hearts, be all love and all glory for time and for eternity. Amen. *JW*

WEEK SIX

Easter Season

Ashes to Fire Week 12

Sunday: With Jesus and the Disciples (2)

Read the Gospel passage from John 14:15-21, the devotional reflection titled "Living Truthfully," and respond to the discussion prompts in the Reflective Journaling section.

THE MUSIC OF ASHES TO FIRE

Week 12: "Give me Music" (Track 13)

Monday through Saturday of Easter Season Week 6

IN THE MORNING:

A personal daily devotional guide includes prayer, a reading from the Old Testament, the Psalms, the Epistles, and the Gospel for each day of the week.

This week's readings are from Deuteronomy, 2 Kings, Ezekiel, Hebrews, James, and the Gospel of Luke.

Inspirational quotes from men and women of faith keep us in contact with our shared Christian heritage.

IN THE EVENING:

An evening psalm and prayer become preludes to nighttime rest and renewal.

EASTER SEASON–WEEK SIX
With Jesus and the Disciples (2)

A devotional reflection based on John 14:15-21

Read the Gospel passage first, then the devotional reflection that follows. The discussion prompts at the end will help prepare you for Sunday school and small-group sessions.

Living Truthfully

It didn't seem to take very long after Billy Carroll moved into our neighborhood that we became fast friends. We were in the second grade and we were pals. We walked to and from school together and played together after school and a lot of Saturdays. We always looked forward to the end of the school year and those wonderful summer days when our fun would be limited only by the fading sun and the call from our mothers to come in.

Over the years of grade school, we played, talked, studied, and sometimes even fought, but nothing really seemed to threaten our friendship. When we got a little older, we would even become reflective on occasion. We talked philosophically about our families, our different religious experiences, and our friendship. Even though we came from very different backgrounds and in most ways were very different people, we vowed that we would always be friends.

Well, along about the end of junior high and the beginning of senior high, we began to move in some different circles, make different friends, and certainly make different choices about life. By the time we graduated high school, we rarely spent time together. My mother still lives in the same house on East Sherman Street, and I believe his parents still live right around the corner on Grant Street, but I haven't seen or talked with Billy since we left high school, more than thirty years ago. Have you ever experienced that kind of thing in a relationship?

In this Bible passage we are hearing a conversation between Jesus and his friends. It revolves around the question of what will happen now that Jesus is preparing to leave them. How will the disciples maintain a relationship with him when he's physically gone? The question is simple: How do you really know someone intimately who isn't there? The truth is that you and I are in the same situation as these disciples. We are discovering what it means to have a relationship with Jesus in spite of his physical absence.

The beginning of this chapter reveals that the disciples were dealing with separation anxiety, the fear that sets in when someone very important to you is about to go away. Their question is our question, "How can we know?" How can we know that God loves us and that God abides with us? Jesus gave them an answer. He said the way they would know his continued presence would not be through a few religious acts or spiritual moments. They would know his presence by living into all that he taught them, a life surrendered to God and lived consciously in his presence.

That's a good word by itself, but there's more. Jesus went on to say that these disciples would have more than a memory of what once was. They would enjoy a present and real experience of the presence of Jesus in their lives. It would not be a long-distance relationship, even though Jesus was returning to heaven. In fact, there would be a way that Jesus would actually live closer and more intimately with them. How would he do that? It would happen through One who Jesus called the *Paraclete,* usually translated as "Comforter."

It's a wonderful idea. *Paraclete* is about One who comes alongside to comfort, to correct, and to console. This is One on whom we can call for help, One to whom we can appeal. Jesus identified that helper as the Holy Spirit. The witness of Scripture is clear: the Holy Spirit resides in the heart of every authentic believer in Jesus Christ. Therefore, we are not left as orphans in this world. The Spirit of Christ himself comes to take up residence in our hearts and to live in an intimate relationship with us.

Do you realize what a powerful gift this is? Sometimes Christians say, "If only Jesus were physically present with us today, then we'd really have it together spiritually." Wrong. These disciples of Jesus were far more powerful in their witness and more effective in their ministry after Jesus left. Why? Because through the Holy Spirit he came to live within them so that his strength would be made perfect in their weakness.

This is good news by itself, but there is even more. The next question is, "What does this *Paraclete*, the Holy Spirit, *do* to keep that relationship with Jesus so real?" The answer Jesus gave was simple but deep: "He will enable you to live in truth." He is "the spirit of truth." Jesus said just a bit later that "he will teach you all things and will remind you of everything I have said to you." In chapter 16, Jesus said of him, "He will guide you into all truth."

We might ask Pilate's question now, "What is truth?" Jesus said in this Gospel, "I am the Truth." So what does all this mean? It means that having a close, personal relationship with Jesus Christ does not primarily involve some extraordinary religious experience. It does not primarily involve "feeling" close to Jesus. It's about *obedience* to the way of life Jesus modeled for us.

Jesus begins this passage saying, "If you love me, you will *obey* what I command." He ends by saying, "Whoever has my commands and *obeys* them, he is the one who loves me." See the connection? Living in a deep and abiding friendship with Jesus isn't about having him miraculously demonstrate himself to us. It's not about being intellectually or philosophically convinced. It is about living out the commands and teachings of Jesus in every corner of our lives. What commands? "Love God with all your heart, mind, soul, and strength, and love your neighbor as yourself."

Jesus is telling the disciples that their relationship will continue. It won't happen by clinging to a memory or by retreating into their private experience of him. It will happen as they continue to love him by doing his works and keeping his commands.

Someone once said, "To love Jesus is to keep his commandments; to keep Jesus' commandments is to love him." The question that pierces my heart through this passage is, "Am I living truthfully?" When we confess our faith in Jesus Christ as Savior, then the truth is that his Spirit lives in us. The question is, "Are we listening to him? Are we obeying the essential things he taught us about how to live? Do we love him by keeping his commands?" —JR

After reading the passage from John 14:15-21
and the devotional reflection "Living Truthfully,"
you may also want to read the following
related passages:

Acts 17:22-31; Psalm 66:8-20; and 1 Peter 3:13-22

The discussion prompts that follow will help prepare you to participate in your Sunday school class or small-group study. Use your reflective journaling section to record any other insights that come to you as you read the Gospel lesson and the devotional reflection.

DISCUSSION PROMPT #1: JOHN 14

Think of a time when you experienced a significant loss. What or who was instrumental in helping you continue with your life after the loss?

DISCUSSION PROMPT #2: JOHN 14

In this passage, Jesus is preparing his disciples for his departure. What does he tell them to do in order to continue faithful lives after he is gone?

DISCUSSION PROMPT #3: JOHN 14

What different messages of comfort do you hear in Jesus' words in these verses?

DISCUSSION PROMPT #4: JOHN 14

How have you felt the real presence of the "invisible Jesus" in your life?

DISCUSSION PROMPT #5: DEVOTIONAL REFLECTION

Will you accept the challenge Jesus "commands" in these verses? If so, how can you specifically put these practices to work in your life?

REFLECTIVE JOURNALING

_____

_____

_____

_____

_____

_____

_____

_____

_____

PSALM 80 ▪ DEUTERONOMY 8:1-10 ▪ JAMES 1:1-15 ▪ LUKE 9:18-27

MORNING MEDITATIONS

PRAYER—O God, you are the giver of all good gifts and I desire to praise your name for all of your goodness to me. I thank you for sending your Son to die for my sins, for the means of grace, and for the hope of glory, through Jesus Christ. Amen. *JW*

PSALM 80:14a, 17, 19—Turn again, O God of hosts . . . let your hand be upon the one at your right hand, the one whom you made strong for yourself . . . Restore us, O LORD God of hosts; let your face shine, that we may be saved.

DEUTERONOMY 8:5-6 *Keep the Commandments*
Know then in your heart that as a parent disciplines a child so the LORD your God disciplines you. Therefore keep the commandments of the LORD your God, by walking in his ways and by fearing him.

JAMES 1:5-6 *Ask in Faith, Never Doubting*
If any of you is lacking wisdom, ask God, who gives to all generously and ungrudgingly, and it will be given you. But ask in faith, never doubting, for the one who doubts is like a wave of the sea, driven and tossed by the wind.

LUKE 9:18-27 *Today's Gospel Reading*

Those who possess the Spirit as their guarantee, and are rich in the hope of the resurrection, already have a hold on what is in store for them as if it had already come to be.
A QUOTE FROM A COMMENTARY ON CORINTHIANS BY CYRIL OF ALEXANDER

EVENING REFLECTIONS

PSALM 77:6, 11a, 13-14a—I commune with my heart in the night; I meditate and search my spirit . . . I will call to mind the deeds of the LORD . . . Your way, O God, is holy. What god is so great as our God? You are the God who works wonders.

PRAYER—O God, fill my soul with so entire a love for you, that I may love nothing but you. Give me grace to study your knowledge daily, that the more I know you, the more I may love you, through Jesus Christ my Lord. Amen. *JW*

PSALM 78:1-54 • DEUTERONOMY 8:11-20 • JAMES 1:16-27 • LUKE 11:1-13

MORNING MEDITATIONS

PRAYER—Lord of all life and power, through the mighty resurrection of Jesus, you have overcome sin and death to make all things new in him. This is the day you have made; I will rejoice and be glad in it. Amen.

PSALM 78:52, 53a, 54—He led out his people like sheep, and guided them in the wilderness like a flock. He led them in safety, so that they were not afraid . . . and he brought them to his holy hill, to the mountain that his right hand had won.

DEUTERONOMY 8:11, 19 *Do Not Forget*
Take care that you do not forget the LORD your God, by failing to keep his commandments . . . which I am commanding you this day . . . If you do forget the LORD your God . . . I solemnly warn you today that you shall surely perish.

JAMES 1:22-24 *Doers of the Word*
Be doers of the word, and not merely hearers who deceive themselves . . . [and] are like those who look at themselves in a mirror . . . and on going away immediately forget.

LUKE 11:1-13 *Today's Gospel Reading*

The thought is full of unspeakable glory—that God the Holy Spirit can come into my heart and fill it so full that the life of God will manifest itself all through this body which used to manifest just the opposite.   A QUOTE FROM OSWALD CHAMBERS IN *BIBLICAL PSYCHOLOGY*

EVENING REFLECTIONS

PSALM 139:11-12, 23—If I say, "Surely the darkness shall cover me, and the light around me become night," even the darkness is not dark to you; the night is as bright as the day, for darkness is as light to you . . . Search me, O God, and know my heart.

PRAYER—O Lamb of God, give me grace throughout my whole life, in every thought, and word and work, to imitate your meekness and humility. May I go through all the scenes of life not seeking my own glory, but looking wholly unto you, and acting wholly for you, through Christ my Lord. Amen. *JW*

PSALM 119:97-120 ▪ 2 KINGS 2:1-15 ▪ JAMES 5:13-18 ▪ LUKE 12:22-31

MORNING MEDITATIONS

PRAYER—Lord God, send your Holy Spirit to be the guide of all my ways and the sanctifier of my soul and body. Give me the light of your presence, your peace from heaven, and the salvation of my soul, through Jesus Christ my Lord. Amen. JW

PSALM 119:103-104—How sweet are your words to my taste, sweeter than honey to my mouth! Through your precepts I get understanding; therefore I hate every false way.

2 KINGS 2:9b-10b, 11 *Let Me Inherit a Double Share of Your Spirit*
Elisha said, "Please let me inherit a double share of your spirit." Elijah responded, "If you see me being taken from you it shall be granted" . . . As they continued walking and talking, a chariot of fire and horses separated the two of them, and Elijah ascended in a whirlwind into heaven.

JAMES 5:16b-18a *The Prayer of the Righteous Is Powerful*
The prayer of the righteous is powerful and effective. Elijah was a human being like us, and he prayed fervently that it might not rain, and . . . it did not rain. Then he prayed again, and the heavens gave rain.

LUKE 12:22-31 *Today's Gospel Reading*

Learn to associate ideas worthy of God with all that happens in Nature—the sunrises and sunsets, the sun and the stars, the changing seasons. Then your imagination will never be at the mercy of your impulses, but will always be at the service of God.

A QUOTE FROM *MY UTMOST FOR HIS HIGHEST* BY OSWALD CHAMBERS

EVENING REFLECTIONS

PSALM 68:1a, 4—Let God rise up, let his enemies be scattered . . . Sing to God, sing praises to his name; lift up a song to him who rides upon the clouds—his name is the LORD—be exultant before him.

PRAYER—Father, grant me forgiveness of what is past, that in the days to come I may with a pure spirit do your will—walking humbly with you, showing love to all, and keeping body and soul in sanctification and honor, in Jesus' name. Amen. *JW*

PSALM 8 ▪ DANIEL 7:9-14 ▪ HEBREWS 2:5-18 ▪ MATTHEW 28:16-20

MORNING MEDITATIONS

PRAYER—Lord of all life and power, through the mighty resurrection of Jesus, you have overcome sin and death to make all things new in him. This is the day you have made; I will rejoice and be glad in it. Amen.

PSALM 8:1, 3-4—O LORD, our Sovereign, how majestic is your name in all the earth! You have set your glory above the heavens . . .When I look at your heavens, the work of your fingers, the moon and the stars that you have established; what are human beings that you are mindful of them, mortals that you care for them?

DANIEL 7:9-10b   *The Ancient One Took His Throne*
As I watched, thrones were set in place, and an Ancient One took his throne, his clothing was white as snow, and the hair of his head like pure wool; his throne was fiery flames . . . a thousand thousands serve him and ten thousand times ten thousand stood attending him.

HEBREWS 2:9   *He Tasted Death for Everyone*
But we do see Jesus, who for a little while was made lower than the angels, now crowned with glory and honor because of the suffering of death, so that by the grace of God he might taste death for everyone.

MATTHEW 28:16-20   *Today's Gospel Reading*

Just as he ascended without leaving us, so too, we are already with him in heaven, although his promises have not yet been fulfilled in our bodies. Christ, while in heaven, is also with us; and we, while on earth, are also with him.   FROM A SERMON OF ST. AUGUSTINE

EVENING REFLECTIONS

PSALM 24:7-9—Lift up your heads, O gates! and be lifted up, O ancient doors! that the King of glory may come in. Who is the King of glory? The LORD, strong and mighty, the LORD, mighty in battle . . . be lifted up, O ancient doors! that the King of glory may come in.

PRAYER—To you, O God, Father, Son, and Holy Spirit, my Creator, Redeemer, and Sanctifier, I give up myself entirely; may I no longer serve myself, but you only, all the days of my life, through Christ my Lord, I pray. Amen. ***JW***

PSALM 85 ▪ EZEKIEL 1:28—3:3 ▪ HEBREWS 4:14—5:6 ▪ LUKE 9:28-36

MORNING MEDITATIONS

PRAYER—Almighty God, I bless you from my heart. O Savior of the World, God of God, Light of Light, you have destroyed the power of the devil, you have overcome death, and you sit at the right hand of the Father. Be today my light and peace and make me a new creature, through Christ my Lord. Amen. **JW**

PSALM 85:8-9—Let me hear what God the LORD will speak, for he will speak peace to his people, to his faithful, to those who turn to him in their hearts. Surely his salvation is at hand for those who fear him, that his glory may dwell in our land.

EZEKIEL 2:1-3a, 7 *You Shall Speak My Words*
He said to me: O mortal, stand up on your feet and I will speak with you. And when he spoke to me, a spirit entered into me and set me on my feet; and I heard him speaking to me. He said to me . . . You shall speak my words to them, whether they hear or refuse to hear.

HEBREWS 4:14 *Hold Fast to Your Confession*
Since, then, we have a great high priest who has passed through the heavens, Jesus, the Son of God, let us hold fast to our confession.

LUKE 9:28-36 *Today's Gospel Reading*

The person who loves God thinks it enough to please him whom he loves, for no greater reward can be sought than that love itself. The pure religious soul delights in being so filled with God that it seeks pleasure in nothing beyond him.

A QUOTE FROM A SERMON BY LEO THE GREAT

EVENING REFLECTIONS

PSALM 91:14-16—Those who love me, I will deliver; I will protect those who know my name. When they call to me, I will answer them; I will be with them in trouble . . . With long life I will satisfy them and show them my salvation.

PRAYER—Father, accept my imperfect repentance, show compassion for my infirmities, forgive my faults, purify my motives, strengthen my weakness, and let your good Spirit watch over me, and your love ever rule my heart, through the mercies of Jesus, I pray. Amen. **JW**

PSALM 87 ▪ EZEKIEL 3:4-21 ▪ HEBREWS 5:7-14 ▪ LUKE 9:37-50

MORNING MEDITATIONS

PRAYER—Lord God, you have left us your holy word to be a lantern to our feet and a light unto our steps. Give us your Holy Spirit that out of the same word we may learn what your eternal will is and frame our lives in holy obedience to it, to your honor and glory and increase of our faith, through Jesus Christ our Lord. Amen.

PSALM 87:1-3—On the holy mount stands the city he founded; the LORD loves the gates of Zion more than all the dwellings of Jacob. Glorious things are spoken of you, O city of God.

EZEKIEL 3:21 *They Shall Surely Live*
If you warn the righteous not to sin, and they do not sin, they shall surely live, because they took warning; and you will have saved your life.

HEBREWS 5:8-10 *The Source of Salvation*
Although he was a Son, he learned obedience through what he suffered; and having been made perfect, he became the source of eternal salvation for all who obey him, having been designated by God a high priest.

LUKE 9:37-50 *Today's Gospel Reading*

Trying to do the Lord's work in your own strength is the most confusing, exhausting, and tedious of all work. But when you are filled with the Holy Spirit, then the ministry of Jesus just flows through you. CORRIE TEN BOOM

EVENING REFLECTIONS

PSALM 136:23-24, 26—It is he who remembered us in our low estate, for his steadfast love endures forever; and rescued us from our foes, for his steadfast love endures forever . . . O give thanks to the God of heaven, for his steadfast love endures forever.

PRAYER—Now to God the Father who first loved us and made us accepted in the Beloved; to God the Son who loved us and washed us from our sins in his own blood; to God the Holy Spirit who sheds the love of God abroad in our hearts, be all love and all glory for time and for eternity. Amen. **JW**

WEEK SEVEN

EASTER SEASON

Ashes to Fire Week 13

Sunday: With Jesus Preparing for His Ascension

Read the Gospel passage from John 17:1-11 and from Acts 1:1-14, the devotional reflection titled "When Jesus Prays for You," and respond to the discussion prompts in the Reflective Journaling section.

THE MUSIC OF ASHES TO FIRE

Week 13: "He Prays for Me" (Track 14)

Monday through Saturday of Easter Season Week 7

IN THE MORNING:

A personal daily devotional guide includes prayer, a reading from the Old Testament, the Psalms, the Epistles, and the Gospel for each day of the week.

This week's readings are from Ezekiel, Hebrews, and the Gospel of Luke.

Inspirational quotes from men and women of faith keep us in contact with our shared Christian heritage.

IN THE EVENING:

An evening psalm and prayer become preludes to nighttime rest and renewal.

EASTER SEASON—WEEK SEVEN
With Jesus Preparing for His Ascension

A devotional reflection based on John 17:1-11; Acts 1:1-14

Read the Gospel passage first, then the devotional reflection that follows. The discussion prompts at the end will help prepare you for Sunday school and small-group sessions.

When Jesus Prays for You

One of the most encouraging and uplifting experiences of the Christian life is to hear someone call out your name in prayer. I discovered the reality of that early in my childhood. I still remember the impact of hearing my mom or dad pray for me, one of the most intimate and loving things that one person can do for another.

One particular memory is from the fifth grade. I was trying to play basketball with the school team. My coordination and agility at that point in my life seemed to be just enough off to get myself hurt. One day I came home in excruciating pain because my finger had been jammed by the basketball. It was swollen, turning black and blue, but I was being tough about it because, after all, this was a war injury.

By the time we sat down for dinner, my finger was really throbbing and now I was starting to complain about it. So as we sat around the table, my dad began to pray. He prayed for me. He prayed very simply that God would touch my hand and help the pain to be lessened. I completely fell apart and burst into tears. My family thought I was crying because of pain. Truth is, I was crying because there was something about hearing my dad call my name to God in prayer that just got to me.

It is deeply personal when someone prays for us. Somehow the ministry of Jesus himself is made real to us when a friend comes alongside and lifts our need to God in prayer. As meaningful as this is, how much more does it mean to realize that our Lord Jesus also prays for us? Think about this for a moment. Do you suppose that Jesus, the Son of God, knows how to pray effectively? Do you think he knows how to pray within the will of God? And wouldn't it be great to know what Jesus prays for when he intercedes for you?

Thankfully, John gives us some insight into that question in his Gospel. In this chapter we hear Jesus pray for himself, for his disciples, and for us. This prayer is especially significant because it comes in the climactic moment of his life. Jesus knows that the cross is just around the corner. He has been intensively teaching his disciples the things they need to know. These are serious things— life and death kinds of things. Not only is he preparing for the cross and his sacrificial death, but he is also thinking about his departure. He knows he must leave his disciples and return to the Father so that he can make intercession for his church (Hebrews 4:14—5:10).

When someone is about to die, you pay close attention to what he or she has to say. Dying people don't waste their words. It is in this context that Jesus prays this wonderful prayer. It begins, not as a prayer of petition, but as a prayer of adoration and thanksgiving. Jesus and his Father are talking about the completion of the mission God had given him to do, to show us the way to eternal life, the way to know God.

Jesus then begins to pray for the believing community. He prays for his disciples and also for us, "all who would believe through their message." I don't know about you, but when I hear Jesus call my name in prayer, I want to lean in and listen carefully to what he prays. I sense that here is where real life is found.

When Jesus prays for us, what does he pray for? He gives voice to a number of things here, but there is one idea, one prayer that seems to lay at the very heart of this intercession for us. Jesus prays that we may be one as he and the Father are one. And this prayer for our unity has a purpose. Jesus desires that we be unified for the expressed purpose that "the world may believe." The most important thing in the heart of Jesus as he prays for us is that we be true to the mission he has given to us, the mission of proclaiming to our world God's love and offer of forgiveness.

Here is where the prayer becomes confrontational. How many times have we done damage to the purpose and mission of Jesus because we refuse to live in unity with one another? The purpose of our unity is not so that we can say, "Look how wonderful we are." It is so we can say to the world, "Look what God is like. The love we share with each other is the love Jesus wants to share with you."

Given this vitally important purpose of our unity, a poignant question presses its way into our minds. Is there anything in our life together as God's people that should ever threaten Jesus' prayer for us? Is there any conflict, difference of opinion, misunderstanding, or personality clash that is worth damaging the mission Jesus has given to us?

The prayer of our Lord that we might be united is not just a nice thing to pray but also what makes us the church. Without this "oneness" we are something other than a community of believers in Jesus. Without this unity we have no hope of influencing the people of this world in any positive way toward a God who loves them.

Perhaps the most important question of all is quite simple. Is the way I live with my brothers and sisters in the church an *answer* to Jesus' prayer or a *barrier* to Jesus' prayer? The power to live in unity is all his. The receptivity to live in this prayer is something that God by his grace has given to us. So what about you?

Are you opening your life to God's sanctifying work, setting yourself apart as his child and as a testimony to the world of what his love is really like? Are you allowing God to work the ministry of reconciliation through your life? Are you living in a spirit and attitude of reconciliation with others? Is there an unforgiving attitude in your heart?

If any of these kinds of barriers are present in your life, then may the prayer of our Lord Jesus be fully answered in you. God in his power will enable you to break down the walls of division and live in forgiveness and reconciliation toward your Christian brothers and sisters. Let's live as an answer to the prayer of Jesus. —JR

After reading the passage from John 17:1-11 and the devotional reflection "When Jesus Prays for You," you may also want to read the following related passages:

Acts 1:6-14; Psalm 68:1-10, 32-35; 1 Peter 4:12-19; 5:6-11

The discussion prompts that follow will help prepare you to participate in your Sunday school class or small-group study. Use your reflective journaling

section to record any other insights that come to you as you read the Gospel lesson and the devotional reflection.

DISCUSSION PROMPT #1: JOHN 17

In these verses from both John and the book of Acts, preparation is a dominant theme. In John, Jesus is preparing the disciples for his departure. In Acts, he is getting the disciples ready for the coming of the Holy Spirit. What are the various preparations mentioned in these passages?

DISCUSSION PROMPT #2: JOHN 17

How do you respond to Jesus' prayer in John 17:1-11? Do you find his words confusing, awe-inspiring, comforting?

DISCUSSION PROMPT #3: JOHN 17

What does the truth that Jesus prays for you mean for everyday living?

DISCUSSION PROMPT #4: JOHN 17

How do you feel after reading the angels' admonition, "This same Jesus, who has been taken up from you into heaven, will come back in the same way as you saw him go into heaven" (Acts 1:11)?

DISCUSSION PROMPT #5: DEVOTIONAL REFLECTION

How can you live as an answer to Jesus' prayer?

REFLECTIVE JOURNALING

_____

_____

_____

_____

_____

_____

_____

_____

_____

PSALM 89:1-18 ▪ **EZEKIEL 3:22-27** ▪ **HEBREWS 6:1-12** ▪ **LUKE 9:51-62**

MORNING MEDITATIONS

PRAYER—O God, you are the giver of all good gifts and I desire to praise your name for all of your goodness to me. I thank you for sending your Son to die for my sins, for the means of grace, and for the hope of glory, through Jesus Christ. Amen. *JW*

PSALM 89:14-15—Righteousness and justice are the foundation of your throne; steadfast love and faithfulness go before you. Happy are the people who know the festal shout, who walk, O LORD, in the light of your countenance.

EZEKIEL 3:22a, 23-24a *The Hand of the Lord Was upon Me*
Then the hand of the LORD was upon me . . . I rose up and went out into the valley; and the glory of the LORD stood there . . . and I fell on my face. The spirit entered into me, and set me on my feet; and he spoke with me.

HEBREWS 6:10-11 *The Full Assurance of Hope*
For God is not unjust; he will not overlook your work and the love that you showed for his sake in serving the saints . . . And we want each one of you to show the same diligence so as to realize the full assurance of hope to the very end.

LUKE 9:51-62 *Today's Gospel Reading*

> The times are too tragic, God's sorrow is too great, humanity's night is too dark, the Cross is too glorious for us to live as we have lived, in anything short of holy obedience.
>
> FROM *A TESTAMENT OF DEVOTION* BY THOMAS R. KELLY

EVENING REFLECTIONS

PSALM 89:19a, 26, 28—Then you spoke in a vision to your faithful one, and said . . . "He shall cry to me, 'You are my Father, my God, and the Rock of my salvation!'" . . . Forever, I will keep my steadfast love for him, and my covenant with him will stand firm.

PRAYER—O God, fill my soul with so entire a love for you, that I may love nothing but you. Give me grace to study your knowledge daily, that the more I know you, the more I may love you, through Jesus Christ my Lord. Amen. *JW*

TUESDAY

PSALM 97 ▪ **EZEKIEL 11:14-25** ▪ **HEBREWS 6:13-20** ▪ **LUKE 10:1-17**

MORNING MEDITATIONS

PRAYER—Lord of all life and power, through the mighty resurrection of Jesus, you have overcome sin and death to make all things new in him. This is the day you have made; I will rejoice and be glad in it. Amen.

PSALM 97:1a, 2-3a, 4-5a—The Lord is king! Let the earth rejoice . . . Clouds and thick darkness are all around him; righteousness and justice are the foundation of his throne. Fire goes before him . . . His lightnings light up the world; the earth sees and trembles. The mountains melt like wax before the Lord.

EZEKIEL 11:19-20a   *One Heart*
I will give them one heart, and put a new spirit within them; I will remove the heart of stone from their flesh and give them a heart of flesh, so that they may follow my statutes and keep my ordinances and obey them.

HEBREWS 6:19-20a   *A Sure and Steadfast Anchor*
We have this hope, a sure and steadfast anchor of the soul, a hope that enters the inner shrine behind the curtain, where Jesus, a forerunner on our behalf, has entered.

LUKE 10:1-17   *Today's Gospel Reading*

Rather, let us be ready for all that God's will may bring, with an undivided heart, firm faith and rugged strength. Let us shut out the fear of death, and keep our mind on the immortality that follows death. Let us show that this is what we believe.

A QUOTE FROM CYPRIAN ON IMMORTALITY

EVENING REFLECTIONS

PSALM 94:18-19—When I thought, "My foot is slipping," your steadfast love, O Lord, held me up. When the cares of my heart are many, your consolations cheer my soul.

PRAYER—O Lamb of God, give me grace throughout my whole life, in every thought, and word and work, to imitate your meekness and humility. May I go through all the scenes of life not seeking my own glory, but looking wholly unto you, and acting wholly for you, through Christ my Lord. Amen. *JW*

WEDNESDAY

WEEK 7
EASTER SEASON

PSALM 101 ▪ EZEKIEL 15; 16:59-63 ▪ HEBREWS 7:1-17 ▪ LUKE 10:17-24

MORNING MEDITATIONS

PRAYER—Lord God, send your Holy Spirit to be the guide of all my ways, and the sanctifier of my soul and body. Give me the light of your presence, your peace from heaven, and the salvation of my soul, through Jesus Christ my Lord. Amen. **JW**

PSALM 101:2b-3a—I will walk with integrity of heart within my house; I will not set before my eyes anything that is base.

EZEKIEL 16:60b, 62b-63 *An Everlasting Covenant*
I will establish with you an everlasting covenant . . . and you shall know that I am the LORD, in order that you may remember and be confounded . . . when I forgive you all that you have done, says the Lord God.

HEBREWS 7:1a, 2b-3 *Priest Forever*
Melchizedek . . . in the first place means "king of righteousness"; next he is also king of Salem, that is, "king of peace." Without father, without mother, without genealogy, having neither beginning of days nor end of life, but resembling the Son of God; he remains a priest forever.

LUKE 10:17-24 *Today's Gospel Reading*

The Lord's resurrection filled us with joy on Easter Day; so too his ascension into heaven is the cause of our gladness now, as we commemorate and solemnize the day on which our lowly nature was raised up in Christ . . . to the throne of God the Father.
A QUOTE FROM A SERMON ON THE ASCENSION BY LEO THE GREAT

EVENING REFLECTIONS

PSALM 119:129, 135—Your decrees are wonderful; therefore my soul keeps them . . . Make your face shine upon your servant, and teach me your statutes.

PRAYER—Father, grant me forgiveness of what is past, that in the days to come I may with a pure spirit do your will—walking humbly with you, showing love to all, and keeping body and soul in sanctification and honor, in Jesus' name. Amen. **JW**

THURSDAY

WEEK 7
EASTER SEASON

PSALM 105:1-22 ▪ EZEKIEL 18:1-4, 19-32 ▪ HEBREWS 7:18-28 ▪ LUKE 10:25-37

MORNING MEDITATIONS

PRAYER—Eternal God, my Sovereign Lord, I acknowledge all I am, all I have is yours. I humbly thank you for all the blessings you have bestowed upon me—for creating me in your own image, for redeeming me by the death of your blessed Son, and for the assistance of the Holy Spirit, through Christ I pray. Amen. *JW*

PSALM 105:7-8—He is the LORD our God; his judgments are in all the earth. He is mindful of his covenant forever, of the word that he commanded, for a thousand generations.

EZEKIEL 18:31-32 *Turn and Live*
Cast away from you all the transgressions that you have committed against me, and get yourselves a new heart and a new spirit! Why will you die, O house of Israel? For I have no pleasure in the death of anyone, says the Lord God. Turn, then, and live.

HEBREWS 7:24-25 *He Is Able to Save*
He holds his priesthood permanently, because he continues forever. Consequently he is able for all time to save those who approach God through him, since he always lives to make intercession for them.

LUKE 10:25-37 *Today's Gospel Reading*

Because humanity needed to be cured of its ancient wounds and cleansed of the filth of sin, the only-begotten Son of God became the son of man, lacking nothing of the reality of manhood and nothing of the fullness of divinity.

AN EXCERPT FROM A SERMON BY LEO THE GREAT

EVENING REFLECTIONS

PSALM 105:37, 43—Then he brought Israel out with silver and gold, and there was no one among their tribes who stumbled . . . So he brought his people out with joy, his chosen ones with singing.

PRAYER—To you, O God, Father, Son, and Holy Spirit, my Creator, Redeemer, and Sanctifier, I give up myself entirely; may I no longer serve myself, but you only, all the days of my life, through Christ my Lord, I pray. Amen. *JW*

WEEK 7 ▪ EASTER SEASON   183

PSALM 102 ▪ EZEKIEL 34:11-31 ▪ HEBREWS 8:1-13 ▪ LUKE 10:38-42

MORNING MEDITATIONS

PRAYER—Almighty God, I bless you from my heart. O Savior of the World, God of God, Light of Light, you have destroyed the power of the devil, you have overcome death, and you sit at the right hand of the Father. Be today my light and peace and make me a new creature, through Christ my Lord. Amen. **JW**

PSALM 102:12, 15-16—But you, O LORD, are enthroned forever; your name endures to all generations . . . The nations will fear the name of the LORD, and all the kings of the earth your glory. For the LORD will build up Zion; he will appear in his glory.

EZEKIEL 34:30-31   *You Are My Sheep*
They shall know that I, the LORD their God, am with them, and that they, the house of Israel, are my people, says the Lord God. You are my sheep, the sheep of my pasture and I am your God, says the Lord God.

HEBREWS 8:1-2   *Our High Priest*
Now the main point in what we are saying is this: we have such a high priest, one who is seated at the right hand of the throne of the Majesty in the heavens, a minister in the sanctuary and the true tent that the Lord, and not any mortal, has set up.

LUKE 10:38-42   *Today's Gospel Reading*

For in the darkness and ignorance of this life, he is the light which enlightens the lowly of spirit; he is the love which draws us; he is the sweetening presence; he, man's approach to God; he, the love of the loving; he is devotion; he is piety.

QUOTE FROM *THE MIRROR OF CHARITY* BY WILLIAM THIERRY

EVENING REFLECTIONS

PSALM 107:9, 35—For he satisfies the thirsty, and the hungry he fills with good things . . . He turns a desert into pools of water, a parched land into springs of water.

PRAYER—Father, accept my imperfect repentance, show compassion for my infirmities, forgive my faults, purify my motives, strengthen my weakness, and let your good Spirit watch over me, and your love ever rule my heart, through the mercies of Jesus, I pray. Amen. **JW**

PSALM 107:33-43 ▪ EZEKIEL 43:1-12 ▪ HEBREWS 9:1-14 ▪ LUKE 11:14-23

MORNING MEDITATIONS

PRAYER—Lord God, you have left us your holy word to be a lantern to our feet and a light unto our steps. Give us your Holy Spirit that out of the same word we may learn what your eternal will is and frame our lives in holy obedience to it, to your honor and glory and increase of our faith, through Jesus Christ our Lord. Amen.

PSALM 107:31-32—Let them thank the LORD for his steadfast love, for his wonderful works to humankind. Let them extol him in the congregation of the people, and praise him in the assembly of the elders.

EZEKIEL 43:2, 4-5   *The Spirit Lifted Me Up*
The glory of the God of Israel was coming from the east; the sound was like the sound of mighty waters; and the earth shone with his glory . . . As the glory of the LORD entered the temple . . . the spirit lifted me up, and brought me into the inner court; and the glory of the LORD filled the temple.

HEBREWS 9:13-14   *The Blood of Christ Purifies*
For if the blood of goats and bulls . . . sanctifies those who have been defiled . . . how much more will the blood of Christ, who through the eternal Spirit offered himself without blemish to God, purify our conscience from dead works to worship the living God!

LUKE 11:14-23   *Today's Gospel Reading*

For he is called the Spirit of God, the Spirit of truth, who proceeds from the Father . . . His chief distinguishing name is Holy Spirit. To the Spirit all believers turn for their sanctification . . . He is the source of our holiness, the light of our understanding.

BASIL THE GREAT

EVENING REFLECTIONS

PSALM 33:8-9—Let all the earth fear the LORD; let all the inhabitants of the world stand in awe of him. For he spoke, and it came to be; he commanded, and it stood firm.

PRAYER—Now to God the Father who first loved us and made us accepted in the Beloved; to God the Son who loved us and washed us from our sins in his own blood; to God the Holy Spirit who sheds the love of God abroad in our hearts, be all love and all glory for time and for eternity. Amen. *JW*

PENTECOST SUNDAY

Ashes to Fire Week 14

Sunday: The Comforter Has Come!

*Read the Gospel passage from John 20:19-23 and the
selection from Acts 2:1-21, the devotional reflection titled
"A Different Pentecost," and respond to the discussion prompts
in the Reflective Journaling section.*

THE MUSIC OF ASHES TO FIRE

Week 14: "Spirit Welcome" (Track 15)

Spirit of God, descend upon my heart,
Wean it from earth, through all its pulses move,
Stoop to my weakness, mighty as Thou art,
And make me love Thee as I ought to love.
Teach me to love Thee as Thine angels love,
One holy passion filling all my frame;
The baptism of the heav'n-descended Dove;
My heart an altar, and Thy love the flame.
Frederick C. Atkinson

PENTECOST SUNDAY
The Comforter Has Come

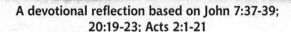

**A devotional reflection based on John 7:37-39;
20:19-23; Acts 2:1-21**

*R*ead the Gospel passages and Acts 2 first, then the devotional reflection that follows. The discussion prompts at the end will help prepare you for Sunday school and small-group sessions.

A Different Pentecost

A few years ago I had the thrill of standing on the south porch of the temple grounds in Jerusalem. Being at this place, which has hardly changed since the time of Jesus, was an emotional moment for me. Many scholars suggest that this was where Peter preached his powerful message on the day of Pentecost.

Most of those in Peter's day who had made the pilgrimage to Jerusalem expected another predictable Pentecost. They anticipated an uneventful return to their daily lives.

But this Pentecost would be different! This Jewish festival was to be the fulfillment of all the Father had in mind when he gave this special feast to his people so long ago (Numbers 28:26-31; Deuteronomy 16:9-12; Leviticus 23:15-25). Like many of us today, these Jerusalem pilgrims were caught up in just "getting by"; they were so focused on *their* living that they had little time for considering the living God. They were so familiar with all the promises of the long-awaited Messiah and the prophecy of Joel (Joel 2:28-32) that the promises no longer fired their imaginations and expectations. They read the words of Scripture as many of us read them today—with appreciation but with little hope that much would come of it.

But this Pentecost would be different. The sun came up. The streets of the Old City were soon filled with people moving here and there in preparation for the day. Many were already praying at the temple. Commercial activity was coming alive. Then everything stopped. There was a sound—a sound like, well, like wind. There was a stirring in the air. And then as soon as it came, it was gone. The people waited a few minutes; nothing happened and they slowly resumed their activities.

But this Pentecost would be different! Locked away in an upper room about 120 praying people were filled with the Holy Spirit in a manner unlike the way they received the Spirit when Jesus had breathed on them, as reported in John 20:22. They were, in the words of Jesus, "baptized with the Holy Spirit" (Acts 1:5) or, as Acts 2:4 says, "filled with the Holy Spirit." They spilled out of that upper room into the streets of Jerusalem, and the world has never been the same. They were never the same. That Pentecost was different!

Let me put it this way. John 1:14 tells us the "Word became flesh and lived among us, and we have seen his glory, the glory as of a father's only son, full of grace and truth." And so it was—thanks be to God!

But on this very different Pentecost the Word that became flesh no longer dwelled simply among the early disciples. Now that Word dwelled *in* them in all his fullness. The world would continue to see his glory, the glory as of the Father's only Son. An incandescent, full-of-grace-and-truth glory for the entire world to see, because the Word-made-flesh now lived his life through these disciples. The good news for us today is that he will express his glory in and through each of us as we, too, are filled with his Spirit!

I have seen him in the lives of those in whom he dwells. My relationship with God has been deepened by people like Patty, Bill, Kiddy, Don, Charlie, Fred, Naomi, Curt, Jim, Paul, Jo, and so many other *real people* whose names I could mention. I have seen Christ living in them, and his grace and truth have become even more real to me through them. That is the miracle of Pentecost—the miracle of a life filled up to all the fullness of God (Ephesians 3:19). It is the wonder of a heart filled to capacity with the love of God.

Paul put it this way in Galatians 2:19-20: "I have been crucified with Christ; and it is no longer I who live, but it is Christ who lives in me. The life I now live in the flesh I live by faith in the Son of God, who loved me and gave himself for me."

Christ lives in me! Christ lives his life in and through me! His message and his mission find expression through my life!

That Acts 2 Pentecost was very different. I don't suppose we will hear any sound like a rushing wind on this Pentecost, and there will probably not be any tongues of fire hovering over those gathered for worship. Yet those were only signs of something far more important taking place in the lives of those early disciples. Acts 1:8 tells us that they received power—resident power in the person of the Holy Spirit. Acts 15:9 tells us that their hearts were cleansed (purified) "by faith."

The question for us today is, "Will this Pentecost be different for us?" It could make all the difference in the world—both in this world and in the one to come. The apostle Paul gave voice to this possibility when he invited the Christians in first-century Rome to yield themselves completely to the Lord:

I appeal to you therefore, brothers and sisters, by the mercies of God, to present your bodies as a living sacrifice, holy and acceptable to God, which is your spiritual worship. Do not be conformed to this world, but be transformed by the renewing of your minds, so that you may discern what is the will of God—what is good and acceptable and perfect (Romans 12:1-2).

May this Pentecost be that life-changing, that transformational, for you! —JKW

After reading the passages from John 7:37-39;
20:19-23; and Acts 2:1-21 along with the devotional
reflection "A Different Pentecost," you may also want
to read the following related passages:

Numbers 11:24-30; Psalm 104:24-34, 35*b*;

1 Corinthians 12:3*b*-13

The **discussion prompts** that follow will help prepare you to participate in your Sunday school class or small-group study. Use your **reflective journaling** section to record any other insights that come to you as you read the Gospel lesson and the devotional reflection.

DISCUSSION PROMPT #1: ALL SCRIPTURE REFERENCES

Looking at all these passages together, what are the images of the presence of the Holy Spirit?

DISCUSSION PROMPT #2: JOHN 7

In the second passage, the invitation is open to "anyone who is thirsty" (John 7:37) to receive "living water" (v. 38), which is a symbol of the Spirit. What does this say about the church's relationship to the rest of the world?

DISCUSSION PROMPT #3: DEVOTIONAL REFLECTION

The devotional reflection includes a reference to John 1:14. Comment on the writer's understanding of this verse as a way to help us understand the wonder and experience of Pentecost.

DISCUSSION PROMPT #4: ACTS 2

When Peter quoted the prophet Joel, "I will pour out my Spirit upon all flesh" (Acts 2:17), is anyone excluded from this promise of God? If yes, who? What would you say to someone who believes the Spirit is only available to some people?

REFLECTIVE JOURNALING

_____

_____

_____

_____

_____

_____

_____

_____

_____

_____

_____

_____

_____

_____

ASHES TO FIRE